COURAGE TO BEGIN AGAIN

Coping With the Loss of a Loved One

by
Olive Ireland Theen

DORRANCE & COMPANY, INCORPORATED
828 LANCASTER AVENUE • BRYN MAWR, PENNSYLVANIA 19010
Publishers Since 1920

To all widows, widowers, and individuals
who must suffer the loss of a loved one,
I dedicate this book.

Contents

Foreword

It is my earnest hope that this book will give comfort and hope to countless individuals suffering from loneliness, grief, and despair after the loss of a loved one.

It fulfills an awesome need. Left to grapple with this monumental, frustrating experience, the bereaved often go into a general decline—depression, apathy, insecurity, loss of faith and health, and even addiction—in order to cope.

In America, friends, relatives, the church, and community have a tendency to leave the grief-stricken alone after the funeral—when grief is most pronounced. Death is and has been a taboo subject, hidden, shunned, and disguised, not a part of life as it should be. This is evidenced by the hospital sending the deceased to a mortuary where he or she is made up nicely, the look of death completely wiped away so the family and friends are spared the awesomeness of the corpse.

Having gone through bereavement, I felt so strongly about this that I took it upon myself to reach out to as many people in the church and community as possible, giving support, care, and friendship. The results were astounding!

Losing a loved one, either suddenly or after a long, drawn out illness, is one of the most devastating experiences one can have. In this and any human relation, love of God can conquer, because God cares. His love is unfailing, His mercy great. Our problems are His problems. We have but to open our hearts to Him, to have faith and trust in His judgments.

The bereaved need help in understanding and thinking through the many emotional and physical problems encountered after the funeral. Everyone is solicitous at the funeral, but afterwards the bereaved are left to work out the grieving alone. People do not come to you, you must go to them for help. This is the general rule, however frustrating it is for the bereaved, who sometimes cannot cope with the changes and problems that follow. It is more important that they be remembered after the funeral. It can hurt when a supportive community appears, then disappears. Help is needed right away, when diverse problems come crashing down on them. They must deal with death, faith, heaven, hell, immortality, as well as health, finances, life itself, the struggle to grow, cutting the ties with the deceased, independence, and new relationships. Faith and love of Jesus is the best way I know to guide the bereaved through the whole process. "The Lord is near unto all them that call upon Him" (Ps. 14:18).

I coped with and survived the trauma by adhering to the Scriptures, accepting God's graces and strengths, and by caring for others. Our Lord bolstered my drooping, sagging spirit many times and gave me hope. "Who trusteth in the Lord, happy is he" (Prov. 16:20).

Thinking back, I can see that a better understanding of the issues involved could have helped me immeasurably during the grieving process. There was so much that confused me. If only I had not doubted and questioned our Lord's wisdom in the beginning—I thought he had abandoned me—I could have saved myself much misery and healed faster. Even when I lashed out with anger, our Lord sustained me. The community disappeared after the funeral, but God did not!

Being brought to grief in one shocking, shattering moment, then crushed with unexpected responsibilities, the bereaved is desperate for assurances to face the grief before rising to new challenges that inevitably come.

In the beginning I had thought that God was unfair to take my husband from me, that He gave me more than my share of disappointments and problems. But trouble is part of life; no one can grow without it. In accepting what God sends, we gain grace, courage, strength, and faith. To know the greatness of God's love we must walk through the valley of the shadows. Life was not meant for temporal but eternal values; not the satisfying of a life on earth, but the development of a life in heaven. This is accomplished by hindrances, not by pleasant methods.

"Behold, I have refined thee, I have chosen thee in the furnace of affliction."

(Isaiah 48)

Looking back, it seems that all the pain and sorrow left me richer than before! I am stronger and can face the world in a kindlier way. Because of my struggle, I can say, "Cheer up, fellow Christian, I went through the affliction and trial. You can too, if you trust in the Lord." Do not the Ten Commandments tell us to love our neighbor? Shouldn't we be workers with God?

In sharing some of these personal experiences with you (always in truth, but sometimes with a bit of humor from blunders and frustrations), it is my sincere wish that you come to know the joy and peace I have known through the love of our Lord, through reading the Scriptures, and through service to others.

"God doeth great things past finding out . . . wonders without number"

(Job 9:10).

1

Reluctant Parting

The last words that I heard from my husband on that stormy January morning a few years ago were "Get the coffee brewing."

Everything seemed perfectly normal. We were enjoying a second cup of coffee while reading the morning paper when my husband, Andy, got up from the table and went back to bed. He was holding his hands over his stomach. Feeling ill at ease, I followed him into the bedroom to see if he was all right. As I was covering him with a blanket, he laid his head down on the pillow and had a massive heart attack. No last words . . . no goodbyes . . . only death!

For a terrifying second, the surprise and shock paralyzed me and left me helpless. "Andy! Andy!" I cried, finding my voice. Then I realized he needed help, so I ran to the phone and called his doctor. The ambulance crew arrived a few minutes later. They could not revive him.

"No, no, no!" I screamed, so terrified I felt like I had been hit by a thunderbolt. As I was reluctantly ushered out of the room, I shouted, "It can't be! It can't be!"

Disaster had struck so swiftly, my mind refused to function. I felt lightheaded, powerless to think clearly, unable even to speak. Stunned by this unexpected, overwhelming blow, I stood in the hallway near the bedroom, dazed, bewildered, and motionless.

"Mrs. Theen," the nurse said, putting her arms around me. "Mrs. Theen!"

Unprepared for so sudden a shock, I was left with an awesome emptiness. A piercing, pathetic numbness took over, leaving me insensitive to my surroundings.

"Mrs. Theen!" the nurse said, ushering me into the living room. "I'll call your pastor and your daughters."

I sat on the couch staring blankly into space—like one in a stupor.

Out of the numbness of my grief came a strange detachment from the scene. The separation somehow enabled me to see clearly. Since I was unable to return to the bedroom physically, I went back mentally. It was as though my subconscious mind would not let me give Andy up. Like in a dream, I beheld the empty shell of the man I had loved, with the repulsiveness of death in all its sordidness—

pale, clammy flesh, open mouth, staring eyes . . .

I came back to reality emotionally drained, shivering, and scarcely able to breathe. I said, "Lord, have mercy!" My inner spirit had taken all the shock it could possibly take. Shaken, the stark reality of death was so repugnant, I could not repeat it even to my girls.

In the difficult hours ahead, without realizing it, God had given me strength and grace to bear the cruel wounds, as well as the upheaval that followed—enough to endure and see to all the funeral arrangements and decisions that had to be made.

Each distraction was like a nightmare. The safe deposit box had to be opened, death certificate made, gravesite picked out, pallbearers called. I attempted to function intelligently, but had to be prodded by my girls into making the right decisions. Now, when I look back, each distraction helped me face the worst day of my life.

Our pastor arrived. His words quieted me. "It is God's will." Then he said, "There is a reason for His taking Andy."

The look I gave him must have cooled his blood. A reason for taking a man from his wife? Surely God could see that I needed my husband on this earth. Feeling wretched and miserable, I desperately needed to break through this stifling mood with some direction, meaning, and purpose. Everything about this day was unreal. My husband dead? It couldn't be true. My Lord would somehow intervene.

But God didn't intervene in the way I hoped. Much later, after I had experienced suffering and trial, He helped me (God doesn't always answer our prayers at the moment, but in other needful ways in His own time).

When nighttime came, I was reluctant to go to bed. Once there, I tossed and turned, pounding my pillow this way and that. Nothing helped. Before falling asleep, I prayed for guidance:

> "Lord, I can't sleep. I am like yesterday's newspaper—shuffled around by the wind, like some kind of a zombie. My soul is sick, emotionally drained. Don't I always depend on you? You said, 'Ask and you shall receive'. My God, you have taken away my husband, and I am numb with shock. What am I to do? I am troubled; my eyes are red with tears. It is hard to accept this death. It is so final. I am haunted by sorrow. It possesses me and I cannot get it out of my mind. You said we should be ready. I hope my husband was ready and is with you now. Amen."

The night was long. I continued to lay awake, pouring out my heart to my Lord: "Now I am a woman incomplete, alone. I do not

2

have the blessed protection and satisfaction of my home. I do not have someone to help and comfort me, encourage and love me. I feel so insecure. My husband is no longer beside me wherever I go, no longer behind me, supporting me in whatever I need to do. It frightens me that I must face the world alone. I am so lonely, blue, and discouraged. How shall I go on living with the memory of this tragic day?"

In a state of semiconsciousness induced by a sedative, I pleaded with my Lord for one last glimpse of my husband:

"Dear Lord, in your goodness and love for me, please let me see
my husband if only in a dream. I need to tell him again that I
love him. I didn't get to say goodbye. Amen."

That night, in a dream I saw my husband standing beside my bed, as natural as life, smiling down at me. Holding out his hand, he said, "Look, Mother, I am just fine. Don't worry!" I was reluctant to let go of his hand.

I awakened from the experience perspiring perfusely, shouting, "Don't leave me! Don't leave me!"

At the beautiful Christian service, I held our pastor's words close to my heart. He said, "It is not darkness where Andy has gone, for God is light. It is not lonely, for Christ is with him. It is not unknown, for Christ is there."

At the gravesite, my mind wandered to a verse by Millay which covered my sentiments so truly:

Down, down into the darkness of the grave;
Gently they go, the beautiful, tender and kind;
Quietly they go, the intelligent, the witty, the brave.
I know, but I do not approve. And I am not resigned.

The icy winter wind cut through the sunshine. During the services, I looked past Andy's coffin at the long line of cars coming to support me and to honor Andy. In an agonizing moment I realized that God could have saved Andy from the sleep of death. My thoughts went back to the passage in John II: "God allows us to go through the agony because in the darkness we learn to believe that He is the Light." This should have sent rays of warmth and comfort to my broken heart. It only saddened me more. Did God, who gives us living hope, understand my tear-stained eyes and aching heart? He said, "I am the way, the truth and the life". Was He now cold and indifferent to my grief? I left the graveside without Andy; without understanding of my suffering. I felt hopelessly and totally drained by this bloodthirsty darkness of death.

At home, friends complimented me on the service. They said he looked nice, so peaceful, like himself. I could have replied, "But you didn't see him in the ugliness of death . . . the face blotched with spots . . . the limp hands . . . coldness of the flesh." The sight is forever stamped on my mind.

A new life awaited me now. How was I going to get along? Almost in a state of panic, my heart pounding, my brain spinning, I knew I was alone and on my own now.

Yet part of my thoughts told me that I was not really all alone. It only seemed so. This was a natural reaction under the circumstances. This was fear. In a more rational moment, a greater power was giving me grace to carry on through the rest of the ordeal. My refusal to accept reality—numbness from shock—eneabled me to bear the cruel wound of the spirit. In the grieving days ahead, God would surely not forsake me if I were to take refuge in His loving heart.

The funeral over, I walked around like a zombie, in a state of unbelief. How could my husband be dead? I never imagined I could be faced with the reality of living with this nightmare. Part of my emotions were still numb—still not accepting reality. It helped when my daughters and I talked about our family, how close we were. We shared memories, touching things that brought pain in remembering: our first baby girl after five years of agonizing waiting— the endless shots, tests, office calls to no avail. Then the prayers were answered! A beautiful little girl was all ours! Months of preparation, sewing clothes, fixing a nursery shortened the time of arrival. My thoughts strayed to the wallpaper that just wouldn't stick to the walls. Andy put on the wrong backing. We laughed and laughed—even took some pictures of the paper falling back on him.

My daughters had to leave for their homes. They urged me to come with them for a while, but I refused.

"I will just have to come back and face it all over again," I told them. "Thanks, but I will stay. Anyway, here is where my heart is. Here is where I feel close to your father. I will be all right."

But after they had gone, I felt so alone, I was tempted to take the next flight out. There was no one to lean on now, no one to love and care about me. I must make all the decisions. There was only stillness—deathly stillness!

4

"Why, God, why?" I kept asking myself. I kept seeing Andy everywhere—in his favorite strato-lounger, reading the paper, smoking his pipe. At noon I kept looking for the car to come around the corner—he always came home for lunch. Then realizing he wouldn't be coming home again, the tears flowed. His bed was empty, his chair at the table empty, the house was no longer the haven it had been. "My Lord," I said, "How shall I stand this pain?" My security, love, partner was gone. All I had left was a lifetime of memories, and I thought, pitying myself, memories won't keep me warm at night or calm my aching heart.

The days were bad enough, but the nights were long and fearful. When I reached over to touch his pillow, I trembled in fear. "Lord," I prayed, "how much longer must I stand this pain? I'm so troubled—sometimes I want to scream. It worries me that I feel this way. I lie awake consorting with self-pity. I bury my head in the pillow, but it insidiously pursues me. When I awake, it clutches me still. I understand that life is full of tribulation, that we all must be battered and bruised—a cross to bear. Then in a more rational moment, I realize that you, Lord, have suffered far more than I, and I am ashamed."

Not all my nighttime memories were filled with self-pity. My thoughts often turned to our Lord. Nothing quieted me like remembering His crucifixion. On a trip to the Black Hills of South Dakota, my family and I enjoyed seeing the Passion Play. As long as I live, I'll never forget the sound of nails being pounded into our Lord's divine flesh! His hanging on the cross—so painful and cruel, all for the love of me and all mankind. He took upon Himself my pain, humiliation, weaknesses, ridicule, and insults so that I might never feel rejected, desolate, or alone in my hour of need! Yes, I am ashamed! I am also human.

In the morning, new obligations and changes must be dealt with—difficult to think about, much less manage efficiently. My thoughts center on how to make sense out of this monumental, frightening experience of losing my mate.

Emerging from the numbness, I lashed out at everyone. Weary, irrational, and shattered, I believed the ambulance was too slow in coming to the house with oxygen and resuscitation. If they had arrived earlier, Andy's life would have been spared. His doctor, too, should have realized Andy's hypertension was much too high. He could have been more alert. And why wasn't I told of his heart condition? And what about Andy's employer? Had he thought only of how much work had to be accomplished? Had he thought about Andy's health?

Bitter, rebellious, and desperate for relief and some answers, I tore into my husband. I thought, If you had cared for me, you wouldn't have smoked so much and worked so hard. You deserted me! You should have taken better care of yourself. Now when I need you most, you have abandoned me, leaving me to fend for myself!

Not only did I blame others; I blamed myself more. I felt that I should have been more sensitive to my husband's tiredness and inertia and not expected so much of him. Wasn't it my responsibility to look after his health? Wasn't it my duty, in accordance with the marriage vows, to watch over him in sickness and in health?

"I failed him," I wailed. "Was it God's will that he died, or failure on my part? If I had been more alert, I would have him with me now. I am to blame." Then I remembered how annoyed I became, just the night before he died, when he had stayed out so late. Like a petty mother hen, I had said, "Your doctor told you to get eight hours of sleep every night. Here it is 2:00 A.M. and you are all wound up!"

The look of hurt in his eyes hurt me now. Why was I so disgusting? He needed recreation as well as sleep. What on earth got into me to reprimand him for such a little thing?

Worst of all, I lashed out at my Lord! Sorrowing, angry, bewildered, I protested, "Wasn't Andy a good husband, good Christian, good provider? If you are a just God and a God of love, why this tragedy? Every morning when I awaken, my heart is filled with hostility. People have disappointed me. How much can I stand? How much can I bear? I feel bruised and defeated. Surely I have had enough. All I want is for you, my Lord, to take all these interminable problems from me and disperse them. I need respite from them."

Probably the hardest thing for me was that I was alive and my loved one was dead. I felt guilty. Sometimes I wanted to suffer to compensate for my so-called lack of concern. Not long after Andy's death, I developed a nervous heart. When it wouldn't go away, I went to my doctor for help.

"It's just nerves," my doctor assured me. "You are experiencing trauma from all your feelings of guilt and anger. You are not to blame for Andy's death."

Little by little my outbursts grew weaker and I cried less. I had always been a sensitive person, but quick to weep. Before I lost my mate, I had enjoyed life immensely. My friends didn't understand my sudden spasms of grief. One even remarked that I should stop feeling sorry for myself. When I heard that, I said to myself, How dare the man! Did he know the anguish of my heart?

After that, I put on a good front. Friends commented on how well I was doing. But I felt shaky. I envied those whose life was intact. I envied couples enjoying each other's company, going home together, while I had to go home to an empty house. I had to get used to being a fifth wheel, single, extra. It hurt. Sometimes I wanted to hurt back. I wanted everyone to understand that I had mixed feelings, that I didn't want to be shut out.

I soon learned that we live in a couples-only society—paired off, man and woman together. There is little room for one alone. One night when I was attending a community affair at my church, I noticed that all the people in the room were couples. My heart leaped, so I ran to the nearest exit. I had to clear away the threatening feelings that seemed to overpower me. This told me that I wasn't ready to deal with my feelings or express them. I could not yet open up or get in touch with my hostilities and anger. I suppressed them. But one day I meditated. It was uncomfortable to let those feelings out and let them surface openly. God understood:

> What time I am afraid, I will put my trust in thee.
>
> (Psalms 56:3)

My confession, which was good for my soul, reflected on the seriousness and dangers to my soul. And I said, "Lord, I acknowledge my fears, insecurity, guilt. Forgive my indiscretions."

The healing of my desolate heart began. God works in wondrous ways!

2

Alone and Comfortless

"Till death do us part," my husband and I had said on our wedding day thirty years ago. Now my hopes, plans, and dreams crashed down on me in seemingly hopeless and irrevocable chaos as death, the great destroyer, closed the door on long years of togetherness.

I didn't realize it then, but my grief work was an up-and-down situation. One day I felt hopeful, the next held a depressing, gnawing void with no real comfort to heal my wounded heart. My cries of despair reverberated around me—loneliness remained. It was like passing through the valley of the shadows.

Frightened, feelings of doubt crept in. All I could see for the future were hindrances and insurmountable obstacles. My immediate need was to find some comfort to offset the loss of my loved one.

In desperation, heartache and misery—irrational behavior if you will—I even envisioned how nice it would be to do as I did in my youth—climb upon Grandmother's knee, feel her holding me tight against her loving breast, then tell me that everything would be all right. But that was impossible since I was a grown woman.

My best possible recourse, at the moment, was my Lord in heaven. Loving, never failing, He would understand my aching heart, jangled nerves, need for comfort, help, and enlightment. I turned to Scripture, chapters 14–16 of the book of John, which told me:

> I [God] will not leave you comfortless.

In spite of this assurance, my spirits remained at a low ebb; my cup runneth over with sorrow. This January day—snowy, blustery, with a temperature of twenty-seven below zero—was hardly conducive to comfort. My thoughts centered on my husband's grave that was covered with sleet and snow. My strength dissipated. I stood in the warmth and dryness of my home and wept. Tears, tears, and more tears flowed freely this day.

During the course of the day my daughter called and cheered me. "Dad is not in that grave," she said. "He is alive in spirit. He is with our Lord."

"If he is alive in spirit," I retorted, "he must be looking down on me, knowing what I am going through."

Later I was to learn that we are often selfish in our grief. That is the reason we are heartbroken and crushed over the "home-going" of our dear ones. We look at our side of the situation instead of theirs. If we could look into heaven and see our Lord, the light and the glory, we would think more of their joy and less of our loneliness. Our dear ones have stepped out of our sight into heaven where they will be waiting for us.

As I was going through a beautiful poem book given me by my next-door neighbor, I ran across a poem that demonstrated all this. Its message was clear: one should get on with life. It was exactly what my husband, a realist, would say. He would tell me not to bother about him. He was released from earth's limitations, and I shouldn't think of his going away but arriving in heaven.

All sorrowing widows and widowers need assurances, some closeness to their deceased members. We don't want to give them up; we want them with us still. The Scriptures comfort us by saying they are angels in heaven.

Maybe I am stubborn, but I didn't understand this new relationship as widow. What did it mean? Why did I feel wounded, bitter, and even resentful being left to fight life's battles alone? I wanted desperately to believe that my husband still wanted to help me here on earth, still cared what happened to me and the children. Questions haunted me. What was my place in all this? Is there life after death? I always believed that our Lord would answer all questions. Then I went straight to the head man, God himself.

Picking up my Bible, I happily discovered that, in the new life in heaven, the dead are able to love, feel, and understand. This new life in Christ is a conscious one, with ability to reason, perceive, and understand. What wonderful news!

As proof of life after death, Christ said to the thief hanging beside Him on the cross, "This day thou shalt be with me in paradise."

Reading further, chapter 15, verses 42–49 of Corinthians, Scripture says, There is a natural body and a spiritual body. The spiritual body will be much the same as on earth, but all the imperfections will be made perfect:

> The body is sown in corruption; it is raised in incorruption.
> It is sown in dishonor; it is raised in glory.
> It is sown in weakness; it is raised in power.

God proved His immortality when He rose from the dead and later appeared to His disciples and hundreds of witnesses. (Science disapproves the life-after-death theory, but faith breaks through the barriers of reason. We can believe Christ and immortality because Christ assured us it is true.) There are many who choose not to accept the spiritual hope and belief in the resurrection of the body. I believe they are missing the truth and warmth that only God can give. Christ said:

> Whoever believeth in me shall never die.
>
> (John 11:26)

My trouble was that I was unwilling and slow to accept or relinquish Andy to God's care. I was not trusting God. In spite of my rejection, He was making me stronger each day to withstand the problems I would have to face in the future. It is doubtful that He who had provided for my needs throughout my life, would now desert me in life, and Andy in death. God does not ignore those who are sorrowing and in need. He builds up our resources so we can take care of ourselves. He wants to train us so we will be strong, not shrink when He wants to prove He can give us victory in the midst of trial by giving us the grace to live above it.

Reading further in the Bible, I found that comfort for the grief-stricken is found in many places in the Good Book. In Isaiah, chapter 61, God says:

> I will comfort all that mourn; bind up the broken hearted.

Not long after Andy's passing, I developed auricular tachycardia—fast and irregular heart beat. Due to the excessive excitability in the heart muscle with stretching which occurs in the dilation of the heart, I became convinced that I, too, might die. I stayed in bed and refused to exert myself. Consequently, I became dependent, something I thought would never happen to me. I desired comfort and sympathy. I seemed bent on getting it one way or the other. For a while it looked like I was playing it for all it was worth.

Sometimes people living alone and grieving let their minds run more scared than need be. Tachycardia often hits people who have suffered severe shock, like sudden heart attack or death of a loved one. This was so in my case. I ran scared for a while. This is not to say that tachycardia is easy to bear. Indeed not! While the contractions rage—sometimes for hours—one becomes very tired. There is pain in the chest, back and arms.

I became increasingly discouraged with my affliction. Fear was my own worst enemy. I was ineffectual in dealing with my inner conflict. Consequently, I was panic-stricken whenever tachycardia came on.

How did I control this turbulent heart, being distraught and fearful? I maintained an uncomplaining outward exterior but harbored an inward spirit of rebellion. How could this happen to me when I had alrady suffered so greatly? I could not manifest an attitude of quiet, patient endurance. It is one thing to endure, but quite another to endure patiently.

In my bereaved state, with its deep wounds, along with metabolic changes, I held to emotional self-pity. For a time I relished the consoling and uplifting expressions of kindness from family and friends. I wallowed in it until I realized I had little reason for my sluggish attitude. In my brighter moments—Dear Lord, I have them too—I knew that I must bear my cross. Strength is born in suffering hearts, not amidst joy.

God had other plans for me.

When I went to my doctor for a check-up, he shocked me into action.

"Get out of your bed," he scolded, "and do something with your life. You are not the only one who has lost a mate or had an illness. There is no excuse for playing lady anymore. There is work to be done. Life to be lived!"

I was so angry I wanted to hit him—hard! How dare he speak to me like that? Had he lost a mate or had heart trouble? How could he know the anguish of a lonely widow's heart?

While I knew he was right to be harsh with me, my heart was empty—dry as dust. I was so choked up, I walked right out of the room without another word. "And I probably won't pay his fee either!" I said to myself.

I simmered down a bit on the way home, but was still angry and provoked. I did, however (feeling somewhat guilty), promise myself I would try to act like a more normal human being.

In the days ahead, I had not yet experienced the comfort of God's strength. Still grief-stricken, I was lost in my own world of uncertainties, not knowing in which direction I should go. The life I had lived with Andy had suddenly and abruptly collapsed and was no more. This I realized but would not yet accept.

The one thing that I could hold onto was the fact that Andy was taken care of in heaven. God would not desert him in death, and me in life.

Those who wait for the Lord
will gain new strength:
They will mount up with wings like eagles,
They will run and not get tired,
They will walk and not become weary.

(Isaiah 40:31)

3

Finding a Way

It is with much trepidation that I write this chapter. My reluctance stems from the fact that it is uncomplimentary to me. It is the truth, as all the chapters are, so I must present the bitter with the better.

It was a period of my widowhood that I am not particularly proud of. My only excuse is that I was grieving mightily right after the funeral. I was going through the valley of the shadow, so to speak. Even though there were people around me, I felt utterly alone and miserable. Those who have lost a loved one will understand this. The aloneness was like the time I viewed the original Mona Lisa at the Louvre in Paris. Though there were crowds around me, I was so enthralled with the painting, I saw and heard no one.

The agonizing days and weeks that followed initiated a loss of zest for living. A sense of futility hovered over me, snuffing out hope, draining energy, and suffocating initiative. The littlest effort became the biggest chore. I didn't bother to groom myself nicely because there was no one to appreciate it. I didn't cook meals because there was no one to share them. I didn't dust the furniture because no one would see it. Why go through the effort? What was the point when all I could feel was an emptiness and a great aching void from the tempest of emotions?

My heart heavy with antipathy, I blamed others for this agonizing time. The devil was having a field day. I became picky, critical, finding faults and shortcomings with everyone. The mailman didn't appreciate my telling him to go around my freshly seeded lawn (he had been going through it as a shortcut). I scolded the paper boy when he threw the paper on the landing instead of up by the door. I even upbraided my neighbor for letting his dog do unsanitary things on my lawn.

Our Lord said, "They [in marriage] shall be one flesh." When in good health, we tend to take for granted what we have until it is gone. With the death of a marriage partner there is acute awareness of the disseverment of the "one flesh." With the death of my partner, the dismemberment tore asunder at such a profound level that my hurt refused to yield.

When I look back on those painful, hurtful days, I am ashamed that I could feel so impetuous, so vehement. I did not like myself;

I did not like the way I felt. A long-time friend reminded me that this, too, would pass. "You will be your old, gentle, peace-loving self again."

Worst of all, I criticized my pastor for not visiting me after the funeral when my loss was so great. I learned that he would gladly have come had I asked for help. I picked up the phone several times, but was reluctant to bother him with my problems lest he think me weak and deficient in strength of character.

However, in my grieving, sorrowing, distressed state, I felt that the church should have adhered to the Biblical "visiting of widows and orphans" in their time of sorrow (James 1:27). I was disillusioned because I had counted on their help and comfort to guide me through bereavement. I thought it was an expected service to all parishioners who had lost a loved one.

I discovered the church had no program of rehabilitation, no kind words to lessen my loss and loneliness. I was forgotten, and my cries were heard only by the walls of my home. I asked, Must I work out my grief alone when the church is competent to deal with attitudes of grief and how to give long-term support?

Every day I expected someone from the church to visit me, but no one came. I was upset and bewildered by such insensitive treatment in the days and weeks that followed. I found it hard to excuse this complete lack of concern. Where was the church's "going about doing good?" (I learned that I was not the exception, but the rule. Most churches help the bereaved after the funeral only if asked.)

In the book of James, chapter 2, verse 27, it clearly states:

> Religion that is pure and undefiled before God
> and the Father is to visit orphans and widows
> in their affliction, and to keep oneself unstained
> from the world.

I wondered if the church was so busy with its emphasis on youth and the living religion that it had no time for comforting the sorrowful. Were they, like society itself, paying little attention to the plight of widows and widowers? Were they avoiding the confrontation of death and were they uneasy in the presence of tears and grieving? I should think not. I learned that the church today is a big institution, busy with all phases of life—offering less help. A pastor cannot be all things to all people. Society ignores and denies death. We don't like the church to be insensitive.

My church had meaningful contacts—couples groups—but as a

single, I no longer fit. Events in the church were scheduled for the family—spouses and children—which made me uncomfortable. Programs, picnics, get-togethers within the church put emphasis on the married and the family. What was especially insensitive to me was the fact that the church accepted work from me, but ignored my grieving. I needed to be a part of the programs at this frustrating time.

I was offered platitudes, but not encouragement. I felt my grief should have been worked out through an atmosphere of caring. To improve its attitude, the church should have visited me at least once after the funeral. The clergy, with its knowledge of death, sorrow, and suffering, could have reached out with understanding and compassion for my feelings and expressed genuine sympathy.

Bereavement is always most traumatic right after the funeral. The widow or widower is distraught, confused, and painfully hurting. This is the time for a caring church to act as the Good Shepherd to one of its flock. Like God's love for all His creations:

> The lost and lonely should be looked for, gathered up,
> cared for, and rescued from its sorrow.
>
> (Ezek. 34:11).

The Bible tells us explicitly that no one should walk in darkness, bearing grief alone, but have the light of life through Jesus who is the truth and the light. Now, when I was grieving, I could have been guided by this kindly light, through a direct, caring talk with my pastor.

Maybe grief was harder for me than most. My aloneness was made more severe by the fact that my subconscious mind was still stubbornly refusing to accept Andy's death. I was still not facing reality. My mind was clenched in rebellion. I was living in the past. (With emotional pain, the healing process can begin only when one stops resisting. A closed mind cannot receive anything—not even comfort.)

Along with this, my husband and I were practically relationless. He was an only child; I had only my sister, who was unable to stay with me.

I learned that many people find it hard to relate to those that mourn. They are uncomfortable with tears—grieving is difficult to express. One good friend later apologized for not coming forward. She said, "I didn't know what to say or how to say words of comfort because I was so sad myself."

Most people do not want to hurt your feelings. They say nothing rather than offend. Yet some come right out and boldly proclaim, "Death is strange and unpleasant. It turns me off!"

I came to the conclusion that I must go it alone, muster my own supports and face tomorrow and the new changes in my life without anyone's help. In my sorrow and sensitivity, I quit going to my church.

In those five unhappy, miserable weeks, Sunday became the hardest day to get through. Watching others going to church hurt, but until I understood, I could not be a hypocrite and feel something that I didn't feel, or be something that I am not.

I felt lost without my church and my faith. It had always been the dependable, never-failing force of good in my life, an efficacious remedy for all life's ills. It seemed almost sacrilegious questioning the church. I had always had a firm grip on my religion, which was a special part of my life. I taught Sunday school for many years, which kept me in touch with my Bible. Whenever I had had a problem, I took it to the Lord in prayer. Now, and countless times since childhood, I have prayed:

> Lord Jesus, my soul is heavy and hurting. I turn to you in time of sorrow and unbelief. I stand before you with open heart. You know what I need before I ask it. Help me to understand my problem. Give me grace and strength to overcome it. With your divine help, I cannot fail."
>
> Amen.

After meditating, I felt so much better. If I trust and obey God, He will take care of every situation, no matter how trying. He will enable me to walk with less fear through it. In the days ahead, I held on to the message in the Twenty-third Psalm:

> Yea, though I walk in the valley of the shadow, I will fear no evil, for Thou art with me.

To improve its attitude toward the bereaved in the parish, I felt my church should organize and put into practice a church-oriented "caring" program for the visiting of the grief-stricken parishioners. Because I had gone through widowhood and understood its loneliness and frustration, I wanted to comfort and give love and sympathy to others in need of this service. I felt I should care and be concerned about their emotional and physical welfare at a time when the death of a loved one had so shattered their hopes and dreams.

I understood their crying out, grief, and sorrow. Suffering of this nature is always so shocking and traumatic. Something in me felt a restless need to ease, look after, shelter, and have a responsible regard for those in sorrow. What I do for others, I do for God as well.

I was qualmish about seeing our pastor. I suffered a painful feeling of uneasiness that I may be acting improperly. I hesitated, fearing I was overstepping and infringing upon our pastor's authority in leading his flock. It was difficult to decide. My misgivings disturbed my state of mind; I was not at all confident. Did I have the audacity to make suggesstions to a superior church authority? Would I be taking liberties, or was it my Christian duty to call attention to a problem overlooked by the church?

I braved the visit because I wanted others suffering grief to know there was help, shoulders to lean on in their time of trauma.

I asked our pastor if I could organize a caring program (at the time, a first in my city) to help out bereaved members who needed help after the funeral when the grief is most pronounced. Support groups fill a need but could not take the place of a one-to-one sympathetic, compassionate discussion with the bereaved that a pastor or associate can effectively give.

I explained my mission: "I will keep in touch with the bereaved. I will visit each, offering myself as a listening post. The bereaved need to talk it out. I will give words of comfort to let them know the church, community, and I care about their suffering and loneliness. I will pray with them, let them know they are loved, that Christ is with them in their sorrow.

"In this way," I continued, "faith can be nourished and grow in the community, especially in today's secularized society. It can spread the faith, visiting in the spirit of Christ, helping to live and witness the faith.

"The program will meet the needs of more people in the parish. It will enliven the faith, increase involvement with one another, and help form a pattern of giving and sharing. In reaching out, parishioners will become more aware of the problems of the world, with a desire to do something about them. This love, care, and concern for the bereaved will not only cause people to live justly but turn from their sins as well.

"When people are going through a severe family crisis such as the death of a loved one, an alert, alive, vibrant, and meaningful parish church and community can be a tremendous support for family life—the basic element in society. Families receive support and encouragement from an active, alive parish. As a result of this involvement, people who have lost faith will return to the church, as I did."

However, with kindness and sympathy, I told our pastor that I understood that more is expected of the clergy than is sometimes humanly possible to give. The clergy have their own spiritual, social, and professional limitations. Even when they have time and concern for the bereaved, they are plagued with money management and financial problems, sermons to work out, social and professional gatherings to attend, and youth services to render. The bereaved receive help with grief after the funeral only if they ask for it.

In speaking to other pastors, I found this to be true. They must be everywhere in the community, church, and hospitals. They must serve on committees, youth groups, senior citizen groups, and in the schools. A large share of their time is spent wrestling with financial burdens and money management. They did, however, feel that a program for administering to the grief-stricken was worthwhile and essential.

My pastor, after hearing my suggestions and plans, gave me his blessings and the go-ahead for the program.

The program caught on; most parishes have help for the bereaved.

On one of my visits to a bereaved member of my church, a feeling of contentment, hope, and faith that I had brought comfort to one sorrowing individual made all my efforts worthwhile. A bereaved lady remarked to me, "Just to know that someone cares makes all the difference in the world. I feel I can go on. My burden seems lighter. Thank you for coming."

This work of love, like nothing I had done, helped me to grow and recover from my own grief. I was becoming one in the mainstream of life.

> Your light must shine before all men
> so they may see goodness in your acts,
> and give thanks and praise to your
> heavenly Father.

(Math. 5:14)

18

4

Again the Faith

The greatest test of my patience was the loss of my husband. It left a gaping hole—a wound so deep, it shook my trust in God!

My marriage meant a lot to me. For thirty years Andy had loved me, cared for me, and held me when I needed him. The emptiness and sorrow I felt in the first weeks were the worst of my life. My emotions cried out for an explanation. I lamented, "Why does everything happen to me?"

When misfortune befalls us mortals, we rant and rave, and wonder how a just God could let this happen. I fell into that trap. It was only after much soul searching and the devotion of a friend that I came out of it unscathed.

I had given up going to my church. I didn't listen to the admonitions of my associates concerning my spiritual health. I reasoned that if my church didn't care enough to help me through bereavement, then I didn't care to have anything more to do with it. Anger and frustration pushed me into looking for someone to blame.

God's guidance and graces were there—I didn't accept them. I didn't look to Him for strength, but doubted His love and wisdom. I gave in to sorrow.

During this dark period of my unfaithfulness, I happened to meet a biologist who had also left her church. She wanted me to join her atheistic society which challenged religious knowledge.

"There is no God," she said, "Nor is there life after death. Andy's death was not God's will, as so many would have you believe."

"I am shocked," I said, hurting from such harshness. "This is morbid talk. You sound like you have a vendetta against the Christian Church."

I had to counter this subtle voice of temptation. Her rhetoric seemed to be distorted, twisted, and ungodly. Like the sand in the desert or leaves in an autumn wind, they could not stand against the judgments of God. Self-centered and arrogant, she satiated her own desires irrespective of the hurt it caused me.

Trying to win me over, she again took up her arguments. "Religion," she said, "is full of questions we cannot answer. This chaos called the world has never been explained. We cannot comprehend the mysteries of life and death."

"But we shouldn't speculate on the mysteries of a benevolent God," I said in rebuttal. "In our efforts to explain everything, our faith can be endangered. God reserves many things to Himself. Many are reserved for a time in the future as He sees fit to expose. He understands His own plans—and ours."

"Every living creature," she said, "has a built-in biological clock that controls aging and fixes the length of life for each species. Man is alloted the time of threescore and ten."

"We are mortals," I said, "and eventually must die. We live in a world of death. We cannot escape the persistent reminders of death that we meet in daily life. We build our lives and make our plans with knowledge that earthly life has its terminal point. Jesus is our bridge between time and eternity. Earth's ills are the outcome of natural laws, the effect of natural causes corrupted by sin. Sin entered the world in the Garden of Eden. Death is thereby passed on to us all."

Conflicting emotions stirred within me. I was not ready or prepared to swallow her unchristian, ungodly approach to life. But misery loves company, so I listened with an open mind to such remarks as, "Death is absolute and final. Religion is for the weak and unknowledgable. Anyway, what proof have you, when no one has yet come back from the grave? A wise person should proportion his or her belief to the evidence."

Although I was hurting from neglect of my church, I felt her vengeance and hostility against God and the church was disgusting, unjust, and uncalled for. She had a calm outward exterior, but harbored a secret inward rebellion that frightened me. I was relieved when she left, but saddened by one who was so bitter, unkind, and unforgiving. Most unbelievers try to take advantage of an aching heart, such as mine, and want to deceive the very elect, if they can.

I theorized that such unbelievers must be unloved and unloving, living under trying conditions, needing someone to blame for their inner struggles. Satan, too, was at the helm of her ship, busily creating undesirable trouble for her once God-loving heart.

Even the atheist has arrived at this atheism only on the basis of faith. He is bound to wonder, How can I know? The love between a man and wife cannot be reduced to scientific proof. All friendship is based on faith. We are not a biological accident. God has purpose in bringing us to life.

Her visit raised my ire to such an extent that I fought back with all the strength I could muster. In no way could I accept her unbelief. Since time immemorial, I had believed with all my heart that "the Lord is my strength and refuge" (Psalm 46:11). I had believed it as a child; I believed it as an adult.

She had, however, raised many questions which I needed to straighten out before resuming my relationship with the church. I needed a professional church intellectual. I went to see Dr. Marie Englander, Ph.D., the retired daughter of a clergyman.

When I approached her, she was more than happy to help me. She had been a college instructor and had helped me write my first article for *Delineator Magazine*. She recalled my balking at the study of Darwinism and evolution.

"My dear," she began, "our earthly life was never meant by God to be a place where human happiness could find its fruition. By sorrow and suffering we are nurtured and prepared for heaven. Trials are disciplinary, a test and proof of character.

"Don't you remember my telling you, 'Pleasure doesn't make the man, life requires a stricter plan?' "

In the course of the evening, I got around to asking her about my way—wanting my husband back because he was still so young with many good years ahead of him.

"But that is selfish," she reminded me. "God knows what He is doing. The birthright of every Christian is suffering. Our Lord Himself was made perfect by trial and sorrow. Shouldn't we do the same?

"I'm sure you have heard," she went on, "that life without sorrow would be a sorry life. For 'whom the Lord loveth he chasteneth, and scourageth every one whom he receiveth' (Heb. 12:6).

"You should not lament your husband's passing," she remarked, "In order to have a full life of peace, you must have faith and trust in God and endure your sorrow patiently. Then you will be blessed and rewarded."

In my frustration and anger, I told her, "I am irrational about Andy's passing. It seems such a waste."

"In God's mercy," she pointed out, "He allowed your grief and sorrow, as well as all the storms of your life, as His instruments to tune and temper your soul. The Scriptures explain it simply:

> Behold, I have refined thee; I have chosen thee
> in the furnace of affliction.
>
> (Isa. 48:10)

"Why have I felt so guilty about Andy's passing?" I asked. "I must be at fault since I feel I could have given him better care."

"It is typical of all widows who lose a mate," she answered. "It was not your fault. Knowing you, I'm sure you did your best for him.

"My dear," she said, "God didn't give you grief to punish you. He gave you strength to bear the sorrow. He never gives more pain than you can take."

I remembered that this is so—in Lamentations, chapter 3, verse 32 it says,

> Though He causes grief, He will have compassion
> according to the multitudes of His mercies. For
> He doth not afflict willingly, nor grieve the
> children of men.

"Of course you are brokenhearted," she said, in her motherly way, "because your loved one is gone to his reward. You wanted him with you always. You were thinking of yourself, not him—his joy and safety with God. He has gone into the presence of the light of Christ and is waiting for you. In the Lord's Prayer, don't you say, 'Thy will be done?'

"Your husband has been released from the limitations of this earth. You should not grieve or refuse to be comforted when it will only be a short time until you and yours will join him in God's house of 'many mansions' which He has prepared for you."

Dr. Marie went into her library and brought out a book of verse. In the conclusion of an evening I shall never forget, she read a lovely poem called "Quietness," by Doran, which reminded me to be patient and have faith, that God had a purpose in my life. I have been molded to fill a particular need. It left me feeling at peace with myself.

> "Be still and know that I am God,"
> That I who made and gave thee life
> Will lead thy faltering steps aright;
> That I who see each sparrow's fall
> Will hear and heed thy earnest call.
>   I am God.
> "Be still and know that I am God,"
> When aching burdens crush thy heart,
> Then know I form thee for thy part
> And purpose in the plan I hold.
>   Trust in God.

"Be still and know that I am God,"
Who made the atom's tiny span
And set it moving to My plan,
That I who guide the stars above
Will guide and keep thee in My love.
    Be thou still.

5

A New Role

It has always been my nature to doubt and question issues. I am, by most peoples' standards, a doubting Thomas. I have to see in order to believe, be shown in order to understand.

Many times, during and after the funeral, friends and relatives kept telling me that Andy's death was God's will. At first I let it go, but after a while, when I questioned what had happened to me, I wanted to analyze the reasons. I desperately needed to understand the blow that life had given me. Even with help, I felt mistreated and entertained unkind thoughts.

A friend and one-time college roommate, Alice Pullman, encouraged me to forget my anger, doubts, and return to my faith and accept what God had offered. Like other well-wishers, she didn't understand that I had lost so much.

"No one can be in tune with life," she reminded me, "unless death is confronted. The spirit cannot grow unless it is challenged."

When I lost the anchor that I had always clung to—my husband—all the comforts, promises, and beautiful renditions of the Scriptures escaped my thoughts. No amount of consoling seemed to help; I was still weak and grieving.

Being the wonderful, faithful friend that Alice was, she kept on with her vigil. However, it was not until some time later that she was to help me. Her own family needed her first.

In the meantime, I measured my life by the moans of my heart and the flow of tears. I didn't realize it at the time, but strength came to me because of my sorrow. It induced humility—cut me down to size—and helped rationalize my inner self as well as overcome the mind's inertia, driving my soul to action.

Many people were most kind to me, but it was my grandmother who had understood life's problems. She was not a Ph.D., but a strong-willed, courageous, sensitive woman from the prairie in Minnesota. Through her experiences of suffering and hardship, I gained valuable lessons that stayed with me throughout my life. One in particular helped me overcome much of my grief—and the flow of tears—in the weeks of widowhood. She told me, while I was spending one summer with her, that my tears were the safety valve of the heart when suffering was on it. She meant that sorrow and grief are the prescriptions God gives us to lighten our load and that they give us strength to go on.

In the course of my quest to understand and my struggle to know and grow, I ran across the lines from the work of Milton: "Who best can suffer, best can do." (Great thoughts, nurtured in hardship and sorrow, produce wisdom.)

It is written that when God is about to make preeminent use of man, he puts him in a fire. Were not the Psalms born in the wilderness, and the Epistles written in prison? Does not our will grow stronger when we challenge, unearth, and get to the root of things?

I felt that the "why" of my husband's death, and religion in particular, were not irrational or irreligious. I had always found comfort in my faith; I had always believed that God was just and a God of love. My faith was the faith of a little child. I found refuge and comfort in such endearing passages as, "Jesus loves me this I know, for the Bible tells me so . . . ."

There were many things that troubled me, things I could not accept. One in particular was death itself. I did not accept it as part of life. Many people, even Christians, do not. The Bible says that death follows life. In the olden days we often heard it as, "He or she went to the Father," and "He passed to his reward." Today we say, "There is a season for all things: a time to be born, a time to live, and a time to die."

The subject of death has always been considered taboo. Most people avoid talking about it. Only at funerals is it discussed, and then only halfheartedly. Doctors, nurses, family and friends look the other way. Hospitals tend to separate us from the dying, who are then taken to the mortuary to be made presentable and lifelike. This keeps us from having to confront the ugly finality of death.

Dying is an unpleasant topic, dreaded by most of us. Is it any wonder that society considers the subject taboo? How else can we avoid its terrifying aspects?

I feared death. As a child I had been conditioned by the church to be haunted by it. "The wages of sin is death," the clergy often used in their sermons. Such phrases as "hellfire and damnation" gave me the impression that it was something to be reckoned with and avoided at all cost.

However, as an adult I questioned this portrayal of a loving God as one who meted out damnation, hellfire, and punishment. Instead of the important event that it should always be, death was portrayed as a fearful, hopeless occasion.

My friend Alice came back into my life again. I found my way back to peace of mind and fervent, religious faith through her help. She loved me in spite of my faults. She stayed with me when everyone else left me alone to fight my grief the best I could.

"There is no grief unless there has been love," she told me one day when I was feeling especially low. "It is good to grieve, good to relate to your husband even when there is pain in losing him. It should give you satisfaction to grieve and realize that you loved him. It is a compliment to him."

A little later she said, "Until you meet grief and accept it, you cannot grow out of sorrow."

She was not always complimentary. Sometimes her words hurt: "You are a spiritual dropout—careful about life, but careless about God. Choked by life's worries, you have been occupied with material things to the exclusion of your spiritual growth. You must remember that God gives grief, sorrow, and affliction to scare you into meditating on eternal values. At death's door, you and many people in the world become afraid and reach out for salvation.

"In surrendering to God's will," she reminded me, "you can better face the hurts and blows by being fortified with His grace and strength and walk unscathed through the most trying circumstances. God's grace converts the most blinding sorrows into the most wonderful blessings. Suffering is for our good and God's glorification.

All things work together for good to those who love God.
(Rom. 8:18)

"As Christians we have many impediments to overcome. We are put in the midst of spiritual enemies—the world, the flesh, and the devil. The spirit gains strength every time it fights a battle. Didn't God say that we all would have tribulation on this earth? Yet He says:

Sorrowing soul, I hear your cry; though soul fires rage, I am nigh.

Life was not meant for ease and pleasure. God's divine purpose is to mature and prepare humans for the unending expansion of heaven."

Alice visited me every day. She was so cheerful, I couldn't help but respond to such a delightful companion. How blessed I was! We talked, talked, and talked some more. After each session, her patience and kindness left me feeling more confident, hopeful, and encouraged to pick up the pieces of my life and get on with living. It was like a balm from sorrow.

Yet her visits often riled me. She wanted me to open up and talk instead of listening. One time she lit into me, in a motherly way, saying, "Your grief has been like a painful wound that hurts like hell. But you are strong, healthy, and, I hope, determined to put all this behind you. Your recovery will be slow, but you will recover and become a stronger person. You have lost a great deal— a friend, a lover, and a person to whom you gave your life. Just as a sore heals, so will you."

Another time (I'll remember it as long as I live) she said, "To reach out and grow, get close to God again." She reached over, held my hand, and began praying. After a while, I joined her in saying the most beautiful prayer:

> Our Father who art in heaven, hallowed be Thy name,
> Thy kingdom come, Thy will be done, on earth as it is
> in heaven. Give us this day our daily bread, and forgive
> us our trespasses as we forgive those who trespass against
> us, and lead us not into temptation, but deliver us from evil,
> For Thine is the kingdom, the power, and the glory forever.
>
> Amen.

I needed Alice's support. She, too, had lost a husband. She understood my grief. But most of the people who visited me after Andy's death were so uncomfortable seeing my tears. I felt isolated and stifled in communicating my feelings. They saw only the tip of my sorrow. Alice had a way of getting me into the spirit of living. She understood my feelings. Hers was a twofold endeavor: to help me over the grief and to get me to return to my church.

"Your loss is only temporary," she told me. "God is in His heaven, and all is right with the world. Soon you will join us. Our Lord brings no one into conflicts of life to desert him. Everyone has a friend in heaven. God would not give man dominion over the heavens and earth only to abandon him."

"I am torn two ways," I told her. "I feel guilty giving up my faith—and for the wrong reasons. In my heart I feel I am wrong, but I can't help myself. On the other hand, I stubbornly cling to conflicting emotions that torment me. I wrestle with my conscience, trying to understand the doubts and questions that perturb me and disturb my reasoning. I realize I haven't been thinking and acting normally."

"One crisis is quite enough for a widow to wrestle with," she said. "You have run the gamut of change, changes in every area of your new life which you have had to deal with, and all at once. They are not only distressing and frustrating, but downright difficult."

"My saving grace," I said, "is that I have always believed explicitly in the Bible and Our Lord's words of wisdom. Then why do I question and doubt when I know that the Bible is truth, a reliable, trustworthy, and never-failing standard to live by?"

"It would be nice if you could just talk to God," she said. "Tell Him your innermost feelings, troubles, difficulties—whatever comes to your mind."

She hadn't pushed me, just gave me shoves in the right direction. I was most grateful for her caring, so one day I took it upon myself to pour out my soul to God. I took a giant step in faith; having His love in my heart, the will of God became my chief desire and true center of my being.

Dear Lord, for a long time now—too long—I have been
without your loving care. I have been lost and lonely.
My grief has devastated me to the point where I need your
intervention. I open my heart to you. Help my unbelief.
I hesitate to bring my troubles to you. They must seem so
small compared to other's needs.

Amen.

6

Reaching Out

Having made my peace with God, I was now ready to get on with my life. But I was unsure what the future held for me. How was this widow to begin? I had had no experience dealing with people, other than the immediate family and friends. However, I had lived through the worst of the pain in bereavement—self-pity, tears, frustration, loneliness, loss of zest for life, and self-accusations. My situation was not unique. As my doctor so sternly reminded me, "You are not the only one who has grieved and survived."

One of the attributes of grieving was the awareness of the suffering of others. I now had the experience and a firm conviction that God would send into my life persons at the right time to work out my future. I had the assurance that God was sharing my problem with me. We were on the same course—God and I. He was already answering my prayer for help. His plans for me, and all mortals, were more bountiful than any plans for ourselves.

> God is able to do far more abundantly
> than all we ask or think.
>
> (Eph. 3:20)

I knew that He would bring good to me out of the tragedy of Andy's death. Upon this solid base of assurance, I happily returned to my church.

I believed that good would come from something constructive to do—an economic good perhaps, or the right work for my hands to do. To ease pain, an empty heart needs therapy. The immediate therapy was cleaning out all Andy's possessions—books, fishing and hunting gear, and the clothes in his closet. I remember packing the clothes in a large box for the Salvation Army. When I came across his favorite leather jacket, I couldn't put it in the box. I held it on my lap and thought of the time I gave it to him. I had taken the money from the grocery fund, little by little so that it wouldn't be missed.

For a time, during those busy hours, I could forget the pain. Then a scarf, hat, anything at all among his belongings, would bring a flood of tears, and the pain of losing him would be back. How was I to literally throw away all that was once near and dear to him and to me?

29

Going through the pockets of his suits, I found a check made out to *Field and Stream* magazine for another two years of delightful reading. How rudely death interrupts our plans! There was much more work for my hands to do this day, tears or no tears; his books, magazines, good shoes and clothes must be packed and given to others who could make good use of them.

I was learning, step by painful step, that reaching out to others, opening one's heart to healing, speeded up the process. With the deep injury of the spirit that I had sustained, I should not shut my heart to help. Isolation is not the answer. However, the bereaved person needs periods of solitude for rest and to gain perspective. I did, but in between times I needed the friendship of others, a oneness with others.

In reaching out and growing, I needed to know what I could do to improve my life and the lives of others. I found the secret in a philosophy of living through seeing and experiencing suffering and sorrow in the lives of others, then helping them cope—bringing joy and hope, comfort and love where needed. It was "getting out of me and into others." This adventure in human relationships, given on a regular basis, would give me little time to be lonely or nurse my own spasms of grief.

This came about when I began visiting the sick, lonely, and dying. One day I visited a nursing home in my area. I made it a rule to help those most devastated, most lonely, most needful. One lady in particular, sitting beside a window, looking out at the blue sky, but not seeing it, caught my attention. That faraway look in her eyes told me she needed cheering up. When I asked her how she was, she replied, "I am depressed, bitter about life. I want to understand why I have to be confined to this wheelchair, with arthritis and heart trouble. My cross is heavy. I am only fifty years old."

That visit, and many visits to come, took me out of myself and my own grief. That first day the words of sympathy came tumbling out of my mouth so swiftly, I scarcely realized their calming message. How did I know what to say? Was this the work that God had planned for me—to help others?

"God loves you very much," I told her, with all the sympathy I could muster. "His is a perfect love. The Bible says that suffering is a part of His plan for us. Praise Him for your suffering, then it will become a blessing!"

Then, a little later, I asked her, "Do you think God gives us suffering to keep us close to Him? It is easy to forget Him when life is glad and carefree."

In my efforts to establish a new identity and to reach out to others, I was inspired by an especially patient, tolerant lady who had previously spent a good deal of time helping me over the rough spots of my bereavement. Her philosophy was, People are human; do not condemn them until you have walked in their shoes for a time.

I found this true. Many people go through life lonely, hungering for what it would be such a joy for me to give. I am sometimes afraid to go seeking them out lest I intrude.

I remember a typical case. A lady I had known many years ago had a bout with a malignant growth that had ulcerated and spread throughout her body. I not only took care of her bodily needs but her depression as well. She grew to depend on me for every little thing, and I resented it at the time. I didn't understand her mental block—fear, anxiety and agitation. She was fearful of dying and leaving all she held dear in this world. I tried to sympathize with her crying out and hopelessness. To create a cheerful atmosphere, I gave her as much hope as I knew how to give by praying for her and with her. My attitude was, You are going to make it. However, I'm sure she didn't believe me. I could have understood her apprehension and dread of the circumstances or the panic and irrational behavior that followed. I remember I grew so apprehensive myself that I watched every word I uttered lest I make matters worse. Now I could have given her more positive help.

To fully understand others, we have to go through the hurt ourselves. In my self-pity, I failed to understand that other people did care about me, despite their seeming indifference. They would be hurt to know that I doubted them. Perhaps they think that I don't care about them either.

Life was not meant for ease and pleasure. God's divine purpose is to mature and prepare humans for the unending expansion of heaven."

After I had the courage to open up to them, I found loving concern in my community. (People do not come to you, you must go to them. This I learned the hard way.) They took note of my comings and goings. They observed me in my garden, stopping to ask, "How are you getting along?" Whenever I needed help in fixing things, they willingly obliged.

31

One day, after trying desperately to put the glass in my storm door, I gave up and called my neighbor. He fixed it in record time. I told him, "It's so nice to have a man around the house."

It is a human trait to want to belong, to be needed, included, and to make connections with others. I did not need to be so lonely, so out of things, as I had thought. I learned to fill up the gigantic, aching void at the center of my being by reaching out, not holding back.

However, independent that I am, I didn't like having to call for help; my pride prevented me from asking for favors. Most times I let it go rather than bother someone.

One of the hardest things I encountered was getting around. I had been so used to having my husband take me wherever I wanted to go that I didn't give it a thought about learning to drive a car. As a youngster I drove our old Model A Ford, but gave it up. Now my transportation had to be taxi or bus. I disliked asking neighbors for a ride to church, to shopping, or to the doctor. I felt a hostility toward a few, but did not blame them for my social discomfort. My independent nature told me to stand on my own two feet and take the initiative.

Necessity is the mother of invention, they say. Determined and swallowing my pride, I crossed the street one day to my neighbor's house and asked if they would give me a ride to church on Sunday. They said, "Yes, next Sunday and every Sunday thereafter!"

I was surprised when they opened up and offered even more. "If you need a ride to the store for groceries, we go on Friday nights. You are welcome to go along. Don't be afraid to ask for help. That is what neighbors are for!"

Being a widow—I hated the word—my self-esteem and self-worth often hit a new low in my bereavement days. Handling feelings of being left out, ignored, forgotten, alienated, and cut off from recreations that I previously enjoyed left me bitter and annoyed at times. Being a new statistic, many friends found it difficult to relate to me. They felt awkward and uncomfortable asking me to their homes. I became a fifth wheel—an extra no one liked to deal with. As a result, my input at social gatherings was minimal. Seeing couples together made me feel more alone than ever. It upset me so much, I dropped out of clubs and get-togethers. Under protest, I told them I would be a guest once in a while, but not a permanent member.

Always having to find a partner for me proved to be annoying. Yes, I felt crushed, but being an independent person, I didn't want to put friends in that awkward position. Finding new friends became a problem for a while. To solve my problems, I pushed myself into helping at the church and doing volunteer work.

Luck was with me. At a Christian women's organization I found many friends. But I thank God every day for a special friend He sent me. She has enriched my life in so many wonderful ways, showing me patience, understanding, and encouragement. Without her confidence, my hopes and troubles would be so much different.

At the table, during our luncheon, she introduced herself and asked, "How are you today?" The two of us were sitting alone, chatting about this and that. When I told her that I was a widow trying to find myself, she smiled and said, "Is there anything I can do for you?" Her care and concern endeared her to me. From this meeting on, my life took on a new perspective.

Feelings of grief returned from time to time—it was uncomfortable to let them surface. These threatening feelings were normal for any bereaved. However, they brought tears and sometimes stabbing pains. And I asked, "When will they disperse? When will I be free?"

One day, quite by accident, I surprised myself by catching hold of a threatening feeling. I ran across a large bunch of beautiful cards that Andy had so lovingly given me—they were too beautiful to throw away at the time. At first, upon reading a few, my heart turned over and I felt so sad. Then I thanked God for giving me a good husband. Since I needed the room, I discarded them.

Life must go on. Cutting the ties to my husband didn't mean that he was forgotten or rejected. A life of togetherness and a pattern of many years standing cannot be completely torn away. Andy will always be a part of my life.

The changes in my new life, a rebirth into a life of diverse circumstances, brought an emotional relief, but sometimes made me uncomfortable. Like most, I like familiarity and security and function best when feeling secure. I have accepted living alone. I am a single, an *I* instead of a *we*. The future and its responsibilities are up to me and me alone. This new me, with unlimited human potential and ability for good, brought me a zest for living, a consciousness within me, and an awareness of what I am and what I could be.

Pain, reverses, and tragedies come to all of us. I had been tested. I no longer wonder why my crosses seem so large, so heavy.

My pattern of growth and fulfillment came from my service to others. I feel vital, alive, and happy, especially when I can lend a

helping hand or show a lost someone how much I care. Then I
should

> Build a life of action around today,
> Fill each hour with loving work and pray;
> Let not my thoughts be wasted on tomorrow,
> God will help me face whatever comes
> Of gladness and sorrow.

The author

7

A Weighty Affair

Just when things started looking up, my health took a turn for the worse. My husband's passing had left a deep, piercing wound in my emotional life, which had physical repercusions as well. This soul-wrenching anxiety left me weary. Several problems came crashing down on me that I didn't know how to cope with—finances, planning for the future, making a life alone, and getting to know and understand myself better. Another problem was health. Not only had my life changed, but my body as well.

Like many humans in time of crisis or sorrow, little troubles can become issues that get out of hand. Being alone, I let my health deteriorate for several weeks until I realized my mistake.

The aloneness left me with an "I don't care, what difference does it make" attitude. Consequently, I didn't eat properly. Good nutrition was farthest from my mind. A cup of black coffee now and then during the day seemed to suffice. Breakfast, lunch, and dinner were piecemeal affairs—anything edible was enough to satisfy what little appetite I had. Foods that I needed—carbohydrates, proteins, fats, and minerals—tasted flat and flavorless as dried-up, week-old buns. Where once mealtime was a happy affair with my husband, it was now the loneliest time of the day. About the only thing I enjoyed eating was something sour, like pickles (one would think I had to be pregnant). All this was hardly conducive to a healthy body and mind.

I lost seven pounds in a very short time. My caloric intake was reduced so severely, my energy needs suffered as well, assuring improper fuel for my body. My nutritional deficiencies worked in a viscious circle—I was simply not hungry and too weak to eat properly. I should have been more aware of the importance of good nutrition and the damage the lack of it could do. With the loss of weight, I looked like Mrs. Scarecrow's cousin—skinny, pale and emaciated.

A general weakness prevailed as a result. All I wanted to do was sleep—and forget. Our Lord said, "Come unto me, all you who are weary and I will give you rest." Well, here I am, Lord, lacking in physical vitality as well as strength to resist the strain of loneliness.

Along with the weight loss, my thyroid reared its ugly head again. Having had a thyroid gland removed surgically at the Mayo clinic, I knew it was important to take treatments for it. It could damage the heart, nervous system, and other glands of the body if left untreated. This, too, caused loss of appetite for me.

For a time I held to a self-pity of "no one loves me now, no one cares" attitude. Living alone was a new, baffling, frustrating experience. Granted, I missed my husband very much. It was frightening at times to realize I would never again have the protection of a husband. I knew that spouses sometimes die of loneliness. I could sympathize because I felt that part of me was missing. Longing and desolation can make anyone feel isolated and unhappy. My aunt Helen was a case in point. I remember Grandma saying she died soon after her husband because she missed him so much.

My daughter visited me. She scolded, "This is ridiculous, Mom. Every abuse of health, every imprudence is a draft on life which you can ill afford. I won't feel sorry for you. It is pure self-pity on your part."

Her words stung. I resented being put to task by my own daughter. But I knew she was right. It was just the jolt I needed. I promised to do better. Before she left, I was on a high protein diet, with lots of fruits and vegetables.

But maintaining sound salubrious health became a real chore. At first, the flat, dull, unsavory, and tasteless foods refused to titillate my taste buds. The cluster of cells at the base of the papillae of the tongue only succumbed when I teased them with savory morsels. Little by little, however, my hunger grew.

Inspired by my new attitude and desire to become my old self again, I attended a cooking school. The demonstrator's opening remark gave me a lift. She said, "Please your family. Each simple food can become an elegant delight if you use extra touches, making taste worth a hundred compliments."

I didn't have a family to cook for, but I could please myself. It was worth it to feel well and look good.

The experience proved rewarding. I not only put extra touches on my own foods but served tasteful, flavorful, savory foods to my guests. Compliments came my way. One lady remarked, "I am inspired by your thoughtfulness and excellent presentation. Your dinner reflects your good taste."

Like all good things, we mortals sometimes go from one extreme to another—like going from the frying pan into the fire, so to speak. In looking back, I can only feel mortified at my inadequate reasoning and behavior.

Once I started eating well again, food became so tasty and yummy, I consumed much too much, sometimes gorging myself—mostly on sweets for quick energy. My appetite was voracious, out of control!

Not only did I have the hungries, but my binge control was nil. Along with that, the magazine ads espoused this food and that as scrumptious: "Satisfy your sweet tooth, keep your own shape; bake yourself happy with a luscious snackin' cake."

Alas! The battle of the bulge was on. The goodies didn't keep me "fit and trim" as the magazines espoused. I didn't become obese or overweight—just overnourished! That's what I told myself, anyway.

Living alone, eating was my only satisfaction—my only enjoyment. Well, why not, I told myself. I snacked on pies, cake, cookies, eclairs, and candy bars! (I kept a good supply of them in the cupboard and refrigerator).

Weight gain was inevitable. Seven pounds, then ten, then twelve registered on the scale in a very short time. For a time no one noticed because I was only one hundred and twenty pounds to begin with. I chalked the weight gain up to a necessary evil.

Looking in the mirror one day, I was shocked at my new look—tummy sticking out, face rounded and bloated. I looked like a chipmunk with his jowls full. This was not me!

I quit eating the sweets for awhile and lost a few pounds, but went right back to eating again. When I began having trouble with constipation and stomach congestion, I realized my yo-yo dieting was physically and psychologically damaging. My body didn't function well, and I determined to eliminate excessive intake of processed sugars and other products. It was so hard to do!

To start the ball rolling, I took every cake, cookie and candy bar to the garbage can. On the way back to the house, I fought with myself. What had I done? My whole system cried HELP!

The fad diets that I tried were ineffectual and common. I gained back the weight because of the frustration with the diet. It was a case of being so upset, frustrated, and stressful that when I calmed down, I got nervous!

When I went to the doctor for my annual check-up, I told him of my dilemma. He almost laughed me out of the office. He shook his head and said (under his breath), "Why do intelligent people do such things?"

Before leaving the office he said, "Reduce your intake of food below that of the body's requirements for the day, modify your eating habits toward a better lifestyle—in essence, adopt a diet that is permanent, not temporary. But also exercise daily to increase your body's expenditure of energy, then work on attitude, image, and self-concept."

My grandma said it all: overeating and gluttony is sinful.

As a Christian I was not spared tribulation. Rain must fall on the just and the unjust. Our Lord was not interested in coddling me but liberating me for a better life. This discipline strengthened my weakness.

> There's a strength comes when we suffer,
> We grow richer when we fight;
> Every test and cup of sorrow,
> Every hurt and blow of life
> Comes to lead us to the light.
>
> The author

8

A New Woman Emerges

I have cut the ties to my husband. My grief and bereavement is done. I now consider myself an *I*, instead of a *we*.

This does not mean that I have dishonored my husband. He, and the life we once shared, will always be a part of me. I will always remember the good and sometimes unpleasant memories of a life together. Experiences like these cannot be forgotten or thrown away. Because of them, I am a stronger, happier, healthier human being. I have fought the good battle and won a deeper appreciation of what life is all about.

I am healed of grief. Cutting the ties is like an emancipation. Once my grief returned, but now it will not return again. I am developing a new identity. Like Rip Van Winkle, I have awakened from a long sleep. I want to live and work again, be a part of life that is real and worthwhile, uplifting and full of action.

I am grateful to those who gave of their time and trouble to make me whole again. I am thankful and full of praise for God who poured out His grace and strength to influence my actions for the better.

It has been a gradual process within myself. I am becoming a different person than the one in my married life. I am changing from the weak, fearful, shaky, unresponsive, grief-stricken individual to one who is eager and willing to improve and strive for greater human potential. Life must go on. I want to be a part of it all, the gradual rebirth into a life of different and challenging circumstances.

Once, when suffering and sorrow hovered over me like an avenging angel, I had strange, bewildering experiences to contend with and work through. I am now free to choose, at my own time and pace, whatever plans and expectations I wish to encounter. I do not have to measure up to the expectations of others nor work at something that does not appeal to me, or is not in my own best interests.

I expect that problems will arise from time to time with my release from the role of wife to widow. I will have to face new challenges, new obligations, with complications each day. Having done grief work, I am stronger now and competent to respond favorably to whatever transpires.

American society once socialized women to be wives and mothers; now they have alternate identities to attain. Regardless of the complexity of human difficulties, I now have the ability, knowledge, and aptitude at my disposal to deal with them. I have trained myself in new and effective skills, entering volunteer work involving committment and competence. I am happy and satisfied with my new independence.

However, if I am to meet new challenges effectively and reconstruct my identity, I must have self-knowledge—know who I am. Then I can grow as a person, find meaning in life, and go on to greater potential. Shakespeare said: Of all knowledge, the wise and good seek most to know themselves.

Having worked through bereavement to recovery, my identity has changed from wife to widow and then to what it will be in the future. This crisis is not new to me. I have changed from childhood—putting away the things of a child—to adulthood; from single—independent—to marriage and parenthood; from bereavement to widowhood.

In order to relate effectively to others, I have to be in touch with myself—know who I am. Then I can grow, feel, and know what my values are. I am comfortable because I understand myself. Because I am in touch with my feelings, I can make decisions that are right for me—with work, religious, financial, family, and other pursuits.

If I am to become aware of my God-given talents, I must learn to like myself as well as others. The second commandment in the Bible tells us to "Love thy neighbor as thyself." I must know my self-worth to have self-confidence in all areas of life.

In my own case, I have pursued long suppressed desires in art and writing. I didn't have the time during my marriage to devote to artistic interests. Now freedom from past responsibilities enables me to pursue whatever interests I wish.

Since I am alone and have already pursued a career in writing and art, I do not want to remain static, but opt to change and grow in other pursuits, if need be. My possibilities are limitless—being in tune with myself, and capable of enjoying what I do, with hopes for the future.

Living alone has many compensations. I can say this, now that bereavement is over. I have the freedom to come and go as I want; my time is my own. I am not restricted in any way. I can be as flexible, open, and ready to change at any time. I can make my own decisions and choices. I have control over my own destiny.

This new-found freedom of mine is terrific. I am free to be, to do or not to do; respond, set goals, and work toward them. I have freedom to laugh and love again, if I choose. I am the master of my own ship of life. It is good.

Recently my children wanted me to sell my home. They said it was too big for one person. They said I would be free of all the responsibilities connected with it. Since the market value was high, I could more than double what Andy and I paid for it. I could invest the money for a tidy profit.

At this time I chose not to sell. In spite of the extra money which had appeal to me, I trusted in my own judgment —I had faith in my decision. I could live in my home as economically as in an apartment, where I would not have the space to rattle around. My home has always filled a basic need in me—I was without one for so many years. As long as I am comfortable and able to take care of all the necessary responsibilities, I shall keep my "haven from the world."

Not all people know what they want out of life. Not all people are aggressive, creative, and talented. But creativity can be cultivated by everyone. It is the ability to see, feel, be aware, and respond—a capacity to experience people and things about us for what they are, without distortion.

When grief work is done, a widow can be creative in her own way—doing her own thing, at her own pace, if she is alone. If she has the concentration, wonderment, ability, and concern with truth in thoughts and feelings and the willingness to let go of the old for the new, she is "becoming" truly creative.

Widows often ask, as I did after bereavement, How shall I begin anew, start over, face life and its problems?

This is what I have learned to do: do not hurry into anything, but take time to evaluate situations and put into practice attitudes and habits that feel natural and right. Become absorbed in an activity, but make your own choices—not what others expect of you. Listen to your own feelings—what you enjoy. Be honest, even when it means doing something different. Work at developing whatever talent you have or want to have that is important to you.

Change is inevitable—alarming at times. This is your life. If you grow, you will need to understand that nothing need be as it is or was. Have the courage to change and carry through any plans that appeal to you or that stimulate your growth. Growth should not mean doing way-out things to impress others, or being inconsiderate of others along the way.

Experience life to the fullest. Don't restrict your perceptions— look, see beauty and goodness around you. Respond to the world, be alive and perceptive, appealing and sensuous. If you find yourself discouraged about problems that seem insurmountable, try to pep yourself up, give yourself assurance that goals will have to succeed. Be positive about your capabilities.

Find help if and when you need it, either from a good friend, pastor of your church, or a professional counselor. In this day and age, it is not a crime to seek help; it is the sensible thing to do.

Bereavement may be a tragic experience, but it has positive aspects as well. My grandfather used to tell me that nothing is so bad that there isn't something good about it.

In the case of a widow, it means you must start anew, find yourself, reach out for opportunities that will stand you in good stead in the future, be hopeful and more fully what you are.

With a love for knowledge, I talked myself into going back to school to learn more about myself and the world around me. I've always been an avid reader. There was a noncredit course in psychology offered by community education at this time, so I enrolled. This nighttime study in human behavior would surely enlarge my scope of life. It did! I learned to control my feelings (a defect I wasn't proud of), develop composure, as well as understand the logic, views, and causes of things. To be honest, anything that would improve my mentality wouldn't hurt!

Unchecked traits, feelings, and desires had often run the gamut of my emotions. Not now! I could have saved myself a lot of grief if I had had this course before. It was shortly after this that a real benefit came to me. Heretofore I had let others sway me on issues, especially during the grief period when I waas most vulnerable. I now had control, strength, composure to follow through without hassle. I now trusted my instincts and was positive about my capabilities.

My big house and equally big yard had become a worrisome problem. Keeping it shipshape taxed my whole system and took pleasure out of every day. A continuous, aching, painful back as well told me it was time I gave up the place and left the hard work to someone else more suited. Without reservation, I sold my house and moved into an apartment.

I shall not forget the lesson I learned the first day of the philosophy course. My teacher handed out this message.

Do not miss the purpose of this life. Go forward
listening and learning. Trust your instincts. In
your own self lies destiny. Let this truth sustain
you. Hold to your highest aim. Live in deeds, not in
words. What you have found to do, do with all
your might, and do your best.

9

Financial Problems

The hardest, most trying, most exasperating experience of my widowhood was the management of my finances.

When my husband died, I became totally responsible for all financial matters. This mathematic headache came at a time when I was already vulnerable from grief. It threw me into a panic because I knew absolutely nothing about money or its management. How then could I possibly cope? Consequently, the straightening out of my financial affairs and the working out of a suitable bookkeeping arrangement devastated me. I almost worried myself into a state of collapse.

To whom could I turn for assistance? What was my best approach to this awesome problem? While I had only myself to think about, now that the children had married and gone, my fears were nonetheless severe. My inability and inexperience in handling money matters trapped me into feeling unworthy.

What made my worry real was the fact that, while I could add, subtract, multiply, and divide, in anything higher than that I was useless. Higher mathematics—logic using special symbols and numbers with rigorous precision—was pure headache. I left it to others whenever possible. I would use my ability to think coherently, form judgments, and draw conclusions in logical matters with subjects familiar to me—English, language, art, history, and music—the beautiful things of life.

There were times when I put a different kind of logic to use— my kind. At a writing class and seminar, I stood before the class and expounded the use of words and thoughts of comfort for all mankind. I learned to use words to inspire daily living and enrich minds by lasting truth and beauty which served to restore souls in the exigencies of life. This was my logic.

My husband had always taken care of the bill paying, account keeping, and other financial details for the family. While I knew we had a checking account, some life, car, health, and house insurance, and a safety deposit box in the bank, I never lifted a finger to take care of it. My job was strictly homemaking and childrearing. That was the way my husband wanted it. (He was from the old school of thought.) The extent of my involvement was writing checks for the grocer and buying clothes for the family.

Now, with the bills piling up at a frightening rate and the Internal Revenue Service practically knocking at my door, I was thrown into an alien situation. Panic is the better word for it!

Statements from the funeral, insurance, and grocer lay unpaid on my desk, reminding me what a failure I was. On top of it all, I no longer had my husband's monthly check to fall back on. In the suddenness of my responsibilities and the confusion with finances, I became concerned. I knew that adjustment was essential to future solvency.

To make matters worse, I was too young for Social Security and too old for the job market. This was made clear to me when I went to apply at the local employment office.

"Whatever am I to do?" I asked myself. My education, though adequate, would not help in business and financial problems that seemed monumental, impossible to straighten out. Caught in a tangled web of inefficiency, my day of reckoning was at hand. This made grief work and widowhood difficult at a time when the morass of social and psychological problems had already taken its toll on my emotional existence. However vulnerable, I knew I had to sort out and come to terms with the situation—and soon!

"Well, old girl," I said to myself, "let me see you get yourself out of this mess!"

Let it be understood, I have never been money-hungry or anxious for material things in general. I wanted just enough to keep things running smoothly. This was putting emphasis on the necessary, not on wrong things. Money being the root of all evil, my thoughts wandered to the passage in the Bible from Luke 12:33:

> Lay up treasures in the heavens that faileth not, where no
> thief approacheth, neither moth corrupteth.

I reasoned that I had surely been endowed with generous treasures and a goodly portion of earth's wonderful gifts. However, I needed to store up a few more dollars on this earth.

An accountant friend came to my rescue. She suggested I start by having good work habits, intensive concentration, perception, and organization. Who, me?

"Bereavement means a big change for you," she volunteered. "You feel uncomfortable because you, like all of us, function best when feeling secure. Many widows suffer financial insecurity. Of course, money cannot compensate for the loss of your loved one.

It can, however, make it easier for you to live well if you learn to save and budget your finances."

In other words, I had to get motivated and stay motivated, have dedication, discipline, and determination. I learned from my grandparents that a winner never quits. "I'll set a goal," I told her. "Then I'll work daily toward my objective of keeping records." (In my lesser moments I wished I could hire a steady bookkeeper.)

I began by studying *Bookkeeping for Today* and using the "T" method—money flowing into my pocket and out of it. There was $145 in my cash account, and $22 that I had paid out. The differences—balance on hand—I added to the right side of the account to make both totals the same. This told me that the "ins" exceeded the "outs". Thank goodness!

But what was my total worth? I needed to understand where to include home, personal, and insurance, as well as my liabilities. Here, too, I had an asset account and a liability account—the received and paid-out entries. All sums received went into the left side column, paid-out sums in the right column. In listing every facet of my existence, I sometimes put the right figure in the wrong column. Along the way, I somehow found my net worth, telling me I was operating properly. What a relief!

My journal, so generously given by my accountant friend, sometimes looked like a tornado has passed through! I opened bills and forgot to post them. It was touch-and-go for a while, but I was learning bookkeeping.

At the end of the month I prepared a profit and loss statement—balances in all accounts—the total of the debits equaling the total of the credits. My balance sheet didn't excite me too much, but I knew where I stood financially.

Just when I was getting a bit proficient, my friend took me to her office where wonderful machines added, subtracted, multiplied, divided, and performed indispensable tasks—machines for every need. (I, who had the greater need, must do it all by hand.)

Learning bookkeeping was not the chore I had assumed, however. In fact, it was comparatively easy. But the nights were far from easy. I dreamed about juggling figures around; numbers raced across my unconsciousness like endless figures on a tickertape.

My education was not finished. Along came the computer, a mind-boggling little monster that could handle routine and repetitive labors. It could balance my checkbook—a chore I detested—keep track of lists and bills, give access to information, and accelerate its transfer. It could check my bank balance, arrange for payment of my bills, and even transfer funds from one bank to another. It was a great little organizer of time that I needed desperately.

This work-from-the-home concept was all well and good, but I needed to get away from the bookkeeping woes. However, one good feature was the fact that if I was tired and the weather inclement, I could send in my sums via the computer!

The cost of this cute little brain staggered me. On my limited budget I couldn't afford it, so it was back to the handwork for me.

Throughout this whole ordeal, I remembered what grandmother used to tell me: "Money cannot bring you happiness." While I couldn't dispute this sage wisdom, hiring someone to do my finances would make me deliriously happy!

My husband had died during a period of hyperinflation. In order to compensate for the high prices and losses, balance my budget, and safeguard future finances, I had to think seriously about saving money along the way. With this in mind, I took my meager savings and invested at a higher rate of interest. I got greater protection by upping the deductible on my insurance. I rode the busses. I bought food when prices were low. Specials saved greatly. Since restaurants were expensive, I made my meals at home, giving myself a treat occasionally to offset the austerity.

My husband and I never thought the day would come when one or the other would have to deal with the death of a mate. We, as others in our culture, put off doing anything until we had to. Now I have learned to know everything pertinent to finances—where documents are, names and addresses of family members, who I can call at a moment's notice should an emergency arise.

I have yet to fully enjoy the fruits of my labors, but the adjustments keep me occupied. I am meeting the challenges and accepting the changes. I must be doing all right. My accountant friend has praised my efforts:

"You are doing well," she said. "Your book work is in good order. You have dealt with the difficult and come through beautifully."

Our Lord never promised joy without sorrow, or peace without pain. He did promise strength and grace for our trials, and undying love.

The Lord is my refuge and strength, a present help in trouble.
(Ps. 46:1)

10

A Talent Awakened

One thing which I had sadly neglected during my married life of husband-caring and childbearing was painting. Being a wife and mother was a beautiful experience but left little time for extracurricular activities.

I hoped and prayed a new career might start for me since I had more time. If I did well, it would give me achievement, advancement, and an occupation whereby I could earn funds to supplement my income. I had to try.

In college art class I had learned to understand art and art forms—basic training, but very little actual experience on canvas. I frittered away my time drawing pictures of children, dogs, and people going by in the street. One drawing of a storm, with trees bending and swaying in the wind, was put on exhibition by my instructor. The students, a bit jealous, said, "Will you look at that? Her pictures aren't that good!"

One day, as I was standing by my picture in the hallway of the auditorium, I saw our college president looking closely at my painting. He had been walking by on his way to giving an address to the students and faculty. He stopped at my painting and said, "Young lady, you have skill and observation. I like it!"

I was delighted and thanked him for his compliment. It was the encouragement I had needed.

However, I was critical of my work. I went on to work in other mediums. I did learn a valuable lesson: the impression the scene makes is more important than the details of reality. The details should be subordinate to the impression of the whole picture.

On the blackboard, in bold letters, our instructor had written: "Fan the tiny spark of possibility into a flame of achievement."

I couldn't have had a more wonderful teacher. She gave us so much of herself. She said, "You must deal with the spirit of a scene, the spirit of nature in your landscapes. Use bright colors for greater beauty. Bring out the delicate shades. Make the manifestation of life your concern—trees living and people breathing. When you have something to say in your painting, be sincere, honest, direct, and have concern for detail. In other words, reveal its innermost beauty."

Our demonstrations of all that we had learned proved interesting.

My painting, a landscape of the city park, was only a rough patch of color, not vivid and graceful, having little appeal to the imagination. To add insult to my already hurt feelings, one student remarked, "That doesn't resemble our city park at all!"

On the back of my painting, my teacher wrote:

"You have not captured the moods of the scenes in nature, nor are your colors harmonious with nature. Your perspective could be improved upon."

My discouragement was real. "I will never be an artist," I said.

Now, many years later, I had time to devote to making a more productive and interesting life. Besides being aesthetically satisfying, creative work would improve my skills, proficiency, and workmanship in all phases of artistic endeavors. I did have a basic foundation in art.

I was full of doubt at first because it had been so long since I had taken a brush in hand. I had to reawaken any natural talent left in me. I knew that growth always depends on activity. There could be no development without effort. With hope in my heart, I tried again. I enrolled in an advanced art class. This time I meant to make it, if at all possible. Like Abraham Lincoln, I will study and get ready, and perhaps my time will come.

My first work on canvas, an oil, proved mediocre. But I clung to the words of Carlyle, that every noble work was at first impossible.

"You didn't paint with as much forcefulness and detail," my teacher informed me. "Your rhythmic pattern of line, mass, color, and light are much better. Keep practicing; you have what it takes to succeed."

After experimenting with the use of color—primaries, secondaries, neutrals, intermediate, complimentary, and tertiary—we went on to advanced hues, their value and intensity, and the principles of color harmony. Working with pigments—primary and secondary colors of light—I worked out the effects by studying light-absorbing properties of pigments.

All this was fine, but I wanted to get down to some real work on canvas. But first our instructor said, "You must learn how colors stir our feelings. Color creates moods, emotions that excite, stimulate, arouse, reflect or upset us. Blue is a quiet, restful—retreating color—while red is an exciting, advancing color denoting violence, courage, and danger."

49

The fun and work began—experimenting with colors in a medium I could use and enjoy. Working in oil did nothing for me, but I could erase and redo my mistakes right away, before the oil dried.

The embarrassing messes I tried to create on canvas strained the patience of my teacher. Her comments were far from flattering. I took off the oil so many times during creation of a landscape, it looked like a confused madman had bungled the blotchy, hodgepodge into an abstraction. At the end of the semester I had improved. I had learned to search for beauty in flowers, trees, hills, and streams. I could not yet interpret feelings, thoughts, facial expressions, and moods. However, I still had not mastered a good landscape. I worked hard for our next art showing. Two of my works showed promise; I had had to incorporate in them everything I had learned. I was determined to succeed, at least a little bit more than before.

When my two landscapes didn't sell, I daringly hung them in the hallway of the teacher's lounge. One day I noticed they had disappeared. When I entered the classroom, I was told they had sold for fifty dollars apiece! I was thrilled.

My next medium was watercolor. In this I had to be quick and decisive. There is no time for changes after the brush strokes are on the wet paper. There is much preparation and equipment to be put together before one may start to paint. I knew I wouldn't succeed in this medium.

Acrylic painting was just what I wanted. It was like oil in substance, but drying quickly. I liked the feel and texture. This was the medium I could improve upon, experiment with, and produce into paintings of delight and beauty.

In the two years since I started to produce again, my work has steadily increased. I have put the knowledge learned into several works of art which have been pronounced good by experts, both here and in Minneapolis. One painting, "Folded Hands" won first place in national competition.

I have memorized some very good rules that I paint by:

1. Have the right attitude. Believe that good work will multiply achievement. High standards pave the way to better things.
2. Love your work. Put enthusiasm into it. Pour into it intense creative energy.
3. Make your paintings you. Put personality into your work.
4. Express yourself boldly and with purpose. Develop awareness of your possibilities.

5. Select colors of your thoughts—weak or strong, good or bad. Select colors of your emotions—weak or strong, discordant or harmonious. Select colors of your acts—weak or strong, fearful or daring.
6. Set a goal and strive for it.
7. Make the ideal in your mind a reality on canvas.
8. Strive not to get ahead of others, but surpass yourself.
9. Keep trying. Failure isn't fatal.

I incorporate these rules in all my works of art today. I've sold paintings to stores, private owners, and to commercial clearing houses for calendars. While I cannot charge large fees as renowned artists do, I make enough money to pay for my supplies and equipment, as well as a little on the side. As yet it could never supplement my income.

Even if I never have astounding success, the experience itself has given me an appreciation of the beauty, sensitivity, and awareness of my surroundings. Every day I thank my Maker for this abundance. I'm keeping busy, putting grief away.

The poet Keats reminds me:

> A thing of beauty if a joy forever; its loveliness
> increases, it can never pass into nothingness.

11

Understanding Immortality

Most Christians have a need to know that they and their loved ones will be together in the hereafter. I especially needed hope and assurance of being reunited with my husband.

While many accept immortality without question, I needed to reach beyond the hope for more conclusive evidence of life after death. From time to time, during my bereavement, little doubts would creep in. I often asked myself, What is it all about? Is it a case of love, wait and hope? I wanted to believe, in spite of my doubts and fears, that there was hope. I clung to the doctrine of a future life as one would cling to a mother's love. Live without hope? Who can? We believe not because of undefined longings within ourselves, but because we learned as a child that Jesus abolished death and brought immortality to light through the gospel.

I did not fully comprehend the mystery of life and death. But this I knew: all paths end in death. Because of this, I had to know more about this deathless, endless existence where my husband now was. I had doubted because I didn't know the whole of it—the why, what, and where of it, so to speak.

Picking up a book of philosophy, I learned that our hope for eternal life does not come from a longing for a spitirual existence, but grows out of love for life upon this earth, which we have found good. Reading further, I found that the only way to be ready for immortality is to love this life and live it as bravely, faithfully, and cheerfully as one can.

In another chapter I read that death cannot kill that which never dies—the spirit and the soul. One's greatest concern should be to feel God's presence, be stirred by His words, have faith in the invisible, and seek satisfaction in the infinite. One's transition from life to death should be without fear, bitterness, reluctance, or discontent. Life eternal is a peace, happiness, and joy combined in spiritual perfection, the peace after the storm, repose after grief, and joy when the conflict is over. Those who die in Jesus live a fuller, nobler life by the ending of all strife and struggle of this world. They are brought together, awaiting the redemption of the body. Out of the dead, cold ashes, another beautiful life begins.

This epitaph, self-written by Benjamin Franklin for his grave, explains:

> The body of Benjamin Franklin, printer
> (Like the cover of an old book,
> Its contents torn out,
> And stripped of its lettering and gilding.)
> Lies here food for worms.
> Yet the work itself shall not be lost,
> For it will appear once more in a new
> And beautiful edition, corrected and
> Amended by the author.

It is said that man is like a prisoner in a cell until he gives the starved soul within him expression, awaiting the better life to which he is going. A Christian's conquest of death is absolute, it is the last of his struggles into the joyous presence of the Lord. Is not the risen Christ the end for which man was made, with the assurance that the end is within reach of all?

Like so many Christians who put off until they have to, I really didn't understand life and death until I lost my mate. I never gave it much thought. There was too much living, caring, loving, and doing all that was expected of me as wife and mother to delve into it.

Now, in spite of my doubts and fears, I wanted desperately to believe that I would someday—God willing—be with my husband. (All people, since time immemorial, have believed that the soul survives the body. Only the body dies, the soul lives on.) I must therefore cling to the doctrine of a future life with Andy. I do not want to be without that hope.

When I was a child I used to picture heaven as a place all shiny and golden, with jeweled walls and pearly gates. In fact, whenever I was teased about some little sin I had committed, I was told, "St. Peter won't let you through the pearly gates—ever!"

I was haunted by my fear of death. It was portrayed as a ghostly skeleton with a scythe—to be feared. Now, when I think of heaven, I think of all my friends, relatives, neighbors, and acquaintances— saints and loved ones there. Not a place so much, but of the good people that I want to be with when I cross over. All the fear and horror disappears because death is as natural as life.

This was brought home to me as I looked upon the face of death in a dear friend. She told me, "I am tired. I want only to lay my head on Christ's lap and fall asleep." Something beautiful happened just before she died: a look of happiness on her face showed a peaceful transition, without fear or bitterness. She went to sleep in Jesus, awaiting the redemption of the body.

During my bereavement, I learned about the hereafter in a most unusual way. I had the occasion to talk to a friend who had had a near-death experience. Her rare, exceptional experience so clearly explained the reason people have a calm, serene, happy—almost angelic—expression of joy on their faces as they leave this world behind. Upon hearing the discourse, I felt that it must be God's way of enlightening us—conditioning and preparing us for a happier death, rather than a sorrowful, fearful departure into an unknown land.

She spoke of coming into the presence of a "being of light," then going through a dark tunnel into a light. There was no pain or fear. She knew what was happening, but it did not matter. She was leaving her worn-out body behind.

This light appeared to ask questions about the directions of her life—personal communication, with a feeling that the "being of light" expressed love, warmth, concern—and even the quality of her life. The experience had a profound effect on her. She said, "I floated into this pure, crystal clear light, an illuminating white light. It was beautiful and so bright, so radiant, but it didn't hurt my eyes. It wasn't any kind of light one can describe on earth. I did not actually see the person in the light, and yet it had a special identity. It was a light of perfect understanding and perfect love. The thought came into my mind 'Lovest thou me?' It was not actually in the form of a question, but the connotation of what the light said was, 'If you do love me, go back and complete what you began in this life.' All during this time, I felt as though I were surrounded by an overwhelming love and compassion."

This real, uncommon experience was a revelation to me. I was so fascinated, I decided to explore the subject further. It surely would help me understand more fully the hereafter, as well as the extent of God's overwelming love for His people.

In a book by Morton T. Kelsey called *Afterlife*, the meeting of the being of light appears as if all the events, feelings, and reactions of one's life are present. In some cases the highlights of one's life appear while others say they saw everything that ever happened in their lives. Some said there were two ways to assess the value of one's life: Did you learn to love others, and did you acquire knowledge? Some told of being in touch with wisdom and knowledge and sharing in that knowledge—contact with the mind that understands everything. Others described the being of light as Heaven and actually seeing the people in the heavenly place, which is different from earthly life. They did not see or hear them, but knew they were there in a place of beauty, love, warmth, and peace.

But one man told of dying and being caught in an unfortunate state of being—a place of gray, dull, meaningless existence. They were stuck in this place and didn't know where they wanted to be. They were caught in their own hates, desires, and fears. The man found himself tormented in hell:

> "I was revived many times, each time, in spite of physical suffering, I begged to be kept alive and saved from hell. After regaining consciousness, I was able to talk, remembering everything that had happened except the terrifying experience of hell."

The quality of pleasant, heavenly encounters makes it difficult for some people to want to return to ordinary existence—the return is resisted. In the first moments of death, there is a desire to get back into the body, but once they see more of the heavenly place, they resist returning.

There seems to be great frustration in returning to normal life after such an experience. They really want to share what happened, but fear people will think them strange. Sometimes these experiences shake one's confidence and view of the world.

This was true of my friend. She had been respected and valued for her knowledge and expertise in creative endeavors. For a long time after her near-death experience she said nothing, fearing her friends would ostracize her. They did.

However, she felt her life had changed for the better. She told me she had a deeper sense of values, purpose, and meaning to her daily life. Her fear of death diminished. She took life more seriously. She felt that life was a constant process of dying to daily events and rising again.

Evidence for survival after death was so important in the history of the Christian Church that it is included in the Apostles' Creed: belief in the communion of saints—all one with those who have died believing in Jesus. Prayer for and with the dead has been practiced since the inception of Christianity. Beliefs of the Apostolic Church consisted of the immortality of Christ through the resurrection (He conquered death) and the body of Christ which remained whole and ascended into heaven.

I was to understand something of what the being of light meant. One night, after my thoughts had returned to that day at the cemetery when my husband was buried, I had another very real dream: I stood beside the grave but couldn't look down into the cold earth. My daughter stood beside me, saying, "Daddy is not there. Look up and think not of an empty place on earth, but a filled place in heaven where he is safe."

I asked, "If Daddy isn't in the grave, where is he?"

Coming to me from a bright light was a voice which said, "O you of little faith!" When I awoke, I was immeasurably shaken. It was only a dream.

Someday I shall know all that seems strange and hard to bear. Our Lord said, "What I do thou knowst not now, but thou shalt know hereafter." His own words proved immortality:

> I am the resurrection and the life. He who believes in me even if
> he dies, he shall live. Whoever lives and believes in me shall
> never die.
>
> (John 11:26)

I see in the risen Christ the end for which man was made and the assurance that the end is within reach. I will not be haunted by the fear of death. The size of my heaven is the exact dimension of my soul. The hereafter is not a place; it is the eternal in me, because the Kingdom is within me. My only concern will be to feel God's presence, follow His advice, have faith, and be satisfied with the infinite. In God's house are many mansions—innumerably more. I have entered only the first—this world. Christ told us that death is not the end. For me this was the final proof I needed—accepting immortality on faith, because our Lord assured me that this is true:

> Let not your hearts be troubled; believe in me;
> In my house are many rooms; if it were not so,
> would I have told you that I go to prepare a
> place for you? I will come again and take you
> to myself, that where I am you may be also.
>
> (John 14:1)

12

Helping Others

For the rest of my life, my major work on this planet will be devoted to relieving the sorrow and suffering of the sick, bereaved, and dying. This is my blessing, my happiness—turning love into action.

If Christianity is to endure, all those who can must become involved. We cannot expect our pastors and leaders to do it all.

During my bereavement, I understood the needs of others because of my own needs. Are we not blessed when we give of ourselves? In fact, my giving, sharing, caring, and going about doing good was one of the things that helped me overcome my own grief. The Bible (Ten Commandments) implores us to love our neighbor as ourselves. God wants us to make each other happy by doing things for each other.

> We are workers together with God.
>
> (Cor. 3:9)

I discovered that in order to calm the fears, worries, and anxieties of the dying that I visit, I first must have a thorough knowledge of heaven. This means that I must understand all that transpires before I can truly alleviate their suffering. Only then can I bring them hope and strength, be close to them, and help them gain as much awareness before they go into the world beyond. I researched the subject thoroughly. The dying, like the bereaved, want to know about the place they are going. They want to be sure there is resurrection on the other side. Death is an awesome experience for them. It leaves them without security and protection from the dark abyss that threatens them and closes the door on everything near and dear to them. The passage conjures a feeling of dread mixed with wonder and reverence.

Since death is a part of life, not something to be hidden, shunned or disguised, awareness of impending death makes dying easier. But who gives a care about death until he or she has to? Andy and I didn't. (Husbands and wives ought to share the eminence of death so one or the other may be prepared.)

In preparing for a visit, I try to remember that people, unconscious or in a coma, can perceive what I say, do, and feel. They know everything that goes on at the time of their passing. This was brought home to me when a close friend was in a coma. I gave her special attention, putting my arms around her and whispering that I loved her.

"You will come into the presence of God," I said. "He knows you are coming. You will be with others in the Kingdom. You will continue the same growth that you had in this life, but without the pain. You will be given help, love and guidance. You will become an angel of God—a carer of all in His kingdom."

When she regained consciousness, she remembered all that I had said to her!

In helping others meet death, I must first admit that I have fears about my own death. The dying person understands this "sharing" experience and will open up in expressing their own worries and fears. I have to believe there is reality beyond the material world—know God—before I can affect the dying. The best way I found is with prayer, meditation, and knowledge of God's love. I need not despair when I remember that my Helper is omnipotent.

This same preparation helps deal with the bereaved and grief-stricken. They fear death in two ways—outwardly and within themselves. The loneliness and meaningless of death bring them into the presence of the destructive forces that work in us. The bereaved are sometimes more fearful then the dying. They are as concerned aobut themselves as the loved one who has died.

I have found the dying very sensitive and lonely. At a time when life is rejecting them, they want consolation and understanding, someone who cares, who listens and shows genuine concern. Don't we all love those who listen sincerely and warmly?

A friend of mine who is a nurse told me of a man in the hospital who was unable to express his concern for his friend who was thought to be dying. He came to visit every day, greeting his old friend warmly and shaking his hand. But he never talked, he sat by the bed and meditated silently. When his friend was well again, he was told, "You will never know how much your visits meant to me during my illness. Just to know that someone cared made all the difference in the world!"

The process of death is an extremely delicate one. Before I reach out to the dying, I must keep my own fears to myself by acknowledging my emotional needs, then putting them aside. This way I can give of myself—wholly and without reservation. Holding their hand, praying together (especially the Twenty-third Psalm), lessens their pain and fears and gives them a measure of peace.

In striving to help our dying loved ones, it is very important that they understand heaven—the place where they are going. Jesus taught us, in words and actions, that heaven is the kingdom of a loving, caring God who is always present. In His nonphysical (spiritual) place, there is fellowship with Him and His angels.

Most of the people that I visit in nursing homes and in the hospital ask me about heaven, especially those who are dying. Sometimes I read the Beatitudes to them, but most times I try to tell them about heaven. This gives the bereaved and dying assurance and real satisfaction and quiets their longing like nothing else I do for them.

I begin by telling them that the Kingdom is theirs if they accept and seek the loving Father who has provided for them in His "many mansions."

> Where I am, you may be also.
>
> (John 14:2–3)

In Matthew 3:44, it says that the kingdom of heaven is a treasure—a pearl that is worth everything one owns. It provides more than seems possible, meets needs we didn't know we had.

With compassion and care, I say to the patient, "We are lost and sorrowful because we know pain from losing a loved one. We are frustrated because we cannot be what we wish to be. But in heaven, we are healed of sorrow and are comforted. Pain, suffering, and fear are washed away from us. We enter into a new life, soothed and relieved of all misery. The forces that have played havoc with our earthly life, damaged by evil, will be replaced in heaven, because evil loses its deadly powers. Our strength is renewed; we have new energy and drive. All those who go to heaven because of difficulties and suffering will be shepherded by God who will "Wash away every tear from their eyes" (Rev. 21:4).

I further explain that the meek are blessed and shall possess the land. What does this have to do with heaven? God's Kingdom reaches out to earth. God has an interest in everything that goes on. He tries to change things. He seeks to have influence upon this earth. Earth is important to heaven. Jesus warned us about judging heaven by worldly standards. The earth is an inheritance of those in heaven. As heirs, the meek provide the care God wants us to have on earth—to watch over and care for those who die, meet them when they cross over, and help them make the transition into heaven.

Those who "hunger and thirst" to see right prevail often fail on earth, but in heaven they are filled and satisfied. The unfortunate, the poor and deprived, will be satisfied, cared for and loved in heaven:

> The hungry he has satisfied with good things; the rich sent empty away.

(Luke 1:49–53)

I try to explain that heaven is a place of forgiveness, love, and mercy. God is merciful. He said, "Blessed are the merciful, for they shall obtain mercy." Christianity promises free forgiveness and mercy to those who ask for it. That is the essential message of Christianity. People do not have to pay for every sin they have committed—heaven is not a place of retribution. Through misunderstanding, people often judge themselves too harshly, thus driving away salvation. People don't have to suffer guilt. They are forgiven every wrong-doing if they are truly sorry and try to remedy the situation.

It takes courage and humility to ask for mercy. Only as we are loved and forgiven do we understand that this is what God's Kingdom is like. God's mercy is beyond the cherished hopes of human beings. This is the central concept of Christianity.

Those who are pure in heart see God in heaven. At the time of death, human love, though tender and gentle, is only a shadow of God's divine love. In beholding the Father face to face, the dead will see what eyes have not seen or imagined. The beauty and joy of that moment is so exquisite that only the immortal soul, separated from the body in death, could gaze upon it and live.

In the book *You Can't Go Home Again*, Thomas Wolfe, at the age of thirty-eight, when he was close to death, had this beautiful vision:

> To lose the earth you know, for greater knowing, to
> lose the life you have for greater life; to leave the
> friends you loved, for greater loving; to find a more
> kind land than home; and more large than earth . . .

So much of my time with the dying is so rewarding. Most persons, at first fearful of leaving their families and this life, become calm and relaxed when I leave them after a visit. Many tell me, "I am not afraid! I will soon have comfort and rest, joy and contentment with our Creator. I will have perfect peace in my heavenly home!"

Each bedside experience leaves me richer, because I have soothed the distressed, brought comfort, consolation, and hope to ease the grief of those who must leave our earth.

Yet it is Christ, having died for our sins, who brought the greatest comfort.

Joy, O Joy, beyond all gladness
Christ hath done away with sadness!
Hence, all sorrow and repining,
For the Sun of Grace is shining!

(Portals of Prayer)

13

Keeping Busy

Carlyle once wrote that the grand cure for all the maladies and miseries that beset mankind is work; that idleness is perpetual despair.

I had early learned the meaning of good work habits—I had to! My grandma always had sound judgment on pertinent issues as well as a sound course of action whenever the need arose. I remember her telling me, "First you work then you play. That is the order of the day." But Grandpa said, "Work is rewarding and a blessing."

One day I put their sage advice to work. It proved more rewarding than I had planned! I entered a speech contest put on at the school. In the auditorium I told a true story of how Great Granny's potbellied stove blew up. While visiting her one day, I inadvertently dropped a roll of firecrackers into her woodpile behind the stove. While the guests were reminiscing, my poor-sighted Granny put more fuel in the stove, along with the firecrackers!

The banging soon began, then grew louder, sounding like a popcorn popper. The hinged lid on the top of the stove danced up and down, the stovepipe got the jitters, and flames belched into the room.

After the fire was put out, I was spanked soundly and put to bed.

But I won the speech contest. After the teachers stopped laughing, I overheard one say, "She pumped life into the contest and turned an otherwise boring day into an interesting occasion."

Now that I was alone, I had time to be creative. The healing power of work would fill my hours constructively and, I hoped, make time profitable as well as open doors to new opportunities. My writing should uplift, inspire, and entertain.

Someone once said that the best way to do great things was to improve doing little things, putting the uncommon effort into the common task. I must therefore start by putting work and purpose into whatever I produce.

Led by the spirit of God, I promised Him I would write only that which was helpful, uplifting, moral, and inspiring to others. My creative contributions in ministering to human needs must have qualities of purpose, self-discipline, endurance, and love.

While I had some basic knowledge and know-how in journalism, I needed a refresher course. With this in mind, I enrolled in an advanced writing course. This would not only get me started properly but would be, I hoped, a shortcut to success.

As I entered the classroom, a sea of curious young faces stared at me—the only elderly lady among them. As I sat down, I overheard such grumbling comments as "Will you look at her?" and "What is she doing here?" But after I opened up in the discussions, they forgot my wrinkled face and gray hairs.

The first thing we all heard was, "Do you have the determination to conquer difficulties, pour spirit into your work, make your assignments a reflection of your faith, integrity, and ideals?"

Near me, from the audience, came a snide and blistering remark, "I'll bet Grandma does!"

Doing my first assignment, I discovered I had to learn many of the tricks of the trade all over again. My knowledge wasn't as basic as I had assumed. What price forgetfulness!

"This course," said our instructor, "will help you with perspective and knowledge to write accurately, clearly, simply, and tersely. It will develop stern, self-discipline in the use of the right words. Learning to write well, you must possess an open mind, inquisitiveness, sensitivity, judgment, and the ability to see life clearly."

That night and several nights thereafter found me burning the midnight oil studying the six rules of writing that our instructor had given me. "Every prospective writer," she had informed us, must learn to incorporate them into his or her works."

I faithfully digested each one. The sheet of rules, now well crumpled from use, lay on my desk, the guide that helped me write my first published story after so long an absence. I incorporate them in every thing I write:

1. Choose words carefully. Your writing must inspire, encourage, guide, carry weight, and be truthful.
2. Select positive words of the heart, mind, and spirit into effective living—determination, patience, endurance, love and faith.
3. Live by the principle of Nothing attempted, nothing gained, and if you fail, you will fail while trying to succeed.
4. Minister to human needs.
5. Write wisely and well, helping others grow and understand.
6. The gift of thought is more precious than the gift of material things.

Little by little my new assignment began at home, right under my nose. It was the hardest work I had done so far—110 percent inspiration and 90 percent perspiration. It was titled "My Two Miracles," the story of how I gave birth to two children when the doctor said I couldn't have any at all! I sold it to *Today's Family* magazine.

I brought the magazine to the class with me. There was such a hoopla, I had to read the story to the class. From that day on, I was accepted by all the students. They rallied around me, wanting to know every detail of how I got it published.

This was the inspiration and encouragement I needed—and the money helped, too.

For my next assignment, I drew on past experiences. My grandfather used to eject philosophical expressions like, Work never hurt anyone. I showed how work was my blessing and my happiness, the reflection of my integrity, my faith and ideals. I was turning my work into something worthwhile, embodying what I thought, felt, and what I did about it. I called it, "Being A Worker." While I didn't sell it, it did earn an *A* from my instructor.

As with all successes I received, I wanted to thank God.

Dear Lord, in gratitude for your gift to me, I want to share that gift with others. Seeing my duty, and not helping others, is unthinkable, an offense to you. Let me, through words of inspiration and faith, be a builder of a more abundant life through my written words.

Amen

A course in Journalism, however, does not always make a writer. There seemed much to comprehend in order to develop the dormant psychic energy that I possessed, to use the whole potential of my awareness, creating imagination, reception to the thoughts of others, and the ability to master circumstances. The course taught me to prepare a manuscript, have a catchy title, interesting characters, as well as presenting the problem or problems, then solving them. I learned to familiarize myself with editors' and publishers' needs, how to write a query letter, and make an interesting outline. I found that knowledge is necessary; applying it quite another thing.

Our instructor drilled into us, "Your story must come alive; the writer must be alive herself, constantly acquiring fresh thought, guiding and putting spirit into ministering to others. Do your best."

All good thoughts, well expressed, reminded me of my grandfather who brought me up. He used to tell me, "No task is too small to be well done. Words have power—they go on in the lives of others."

A gifted man, he knew and understood the passages in the Bible—even the most difficult. I remember one time he told me that the Sermon on the Mount lifted the spirits of all generations. "Simply written words that express love, faith, courage, and hope have immortal significance. Ideas, ideals, and examples can live forever in the lives of others. They help mankind to grow and understand, merging and influencing others of every age."

I understood that God made nothing so beautiful as words—words that express, inform, command, teach and explain every common thing they touch. Victor Hugo's words inspired us to the sacredness of childhood. Charles Dickens inspired us to the divinity of kindness, Longfellow with hope, and Whittier with human brotherhood. They create for all a world of wonder and challenge. They thank God for opportunities, abilities, talents, beauty, health, strength, and happiness. The Bible speaks truthfully and eloquently of man's giving his natural gifts effective to this world:

> Though I speak with the tongues of men and of angels, and have
> not charity, I am become as sounding brass, or a tinkling cymbal.
>
> (Cor. 13:1)

After the writing course, I settled down to some sober and serious thinking. I asked myself if I could produce words worth the reader's time.

One morning, while having coffee with a friend, I asked, "What shall I write about now?"

Her answer was in tune with my own thoughts. "Write about the things that are familiar to you."

"That's great advice," I said with enthusiasm. "The other successes were about things near and dear to me. I've been thinking about writing another book—this one—about how I coped with losing my loved one."

"Oh, that's excellent," she exclaimed, excitedly. "Go to it and give it all you've got. Out there are twelve and one-half million widows and widowers who are in need, feeling lost and lonely, frustrated, not knowing which way to turn. In their grief, they are emotionally drained, disorganized, having insurmountable problems that cry to heaven for help."

"I'll do it," I said hopefully, knowing all that I had to go through these past months. "I sincerely want to guide others through their grief experiences."

"In doing so," Alice reminded me, "you will be giving them

hope as well as lessoning their misery, pain, and sorrow. God bless you in your efforts."

That night I tossed and turned in my bed, going over the prospects of writing another book. It had been quite a while since I had done so. Could I do it again? Was it needed? Did it have sales potential? Yes, helping others is God's plan for me.

> All that the Lord speaketh, that I must do.
>
> (Num. 23:26)

Bright and early the next morning—I couldn't sleep for thinking about it—I went to my typewriter and "dug in." I made an outline, tore it up, then made another more suitable. Each experience was a separate entity. The hard part was remembering and reliving the trauma all over again. There were jabs of pain, and a few tears here and there. The suffering was good for my soul. When I thought about the help I would be giving to others, it was all worthwhile.

After several tries—mistakes is the better word for it—I had a pretty good picture of what the work would entail. Getting started in the first chapter was the hardest, but one word followed another, and I found my thoughts coming faster than I could put them down on paper. Rusty or not, I was on my way. It felt wonderful creating again.

Once again God had responded to my appeal for help. He reached into my pathetic emptiness and planted objective and purpose there, in a way most beneficial. Truly He watches over His own! There was genuine meaning to my life now.

Days, weeks, and months sped by. I couldn't believe I had accomplished so much. It was hard work—grueling at times. When I finished the first draft, rewriting, changing, adding, and taking away all that was unnecessary began in earnest. Every word had been a joy to write.

> Let me rise up with the sun, let me do what must be done;
> Let me work with steady sway, let me do my best today.
>
> The author

14

New Relationships

Only once since my husband died have I considered remarriage. It was with mixed feelings and trepidation when I became involved with Carl. I knew there would be many obstacles to consider. The problems and adjustments were many: children had to be considered; financial arangements made; grief work and mourning had to be finished; love of the first mate should not dominate one's thinking. Then, too, aloneness had to be accepted, feelings of isolation overcome, and a grown, adult attitude attained.

In my widowhood I had known a wide range of experiences dealing with the second marriages of many friends; many of them with unhappy endings. Just before my own consideration, a relative encountered conflicts with the children of both partners. Objections, hurt feelings, and a great deal of bickering ensued; friends and relatives showed displeasure and began taking sides in the new relationship.

When I met Carl, I thought I had met my match. He was a widower, having lost his wife in an accident. We met through mutual friends and enjoyed each other's company.

While I wasn't looking for a husband, I did enjoy the companionship. We got along very well, liking the same things—music, books, traveling, fishing, and camping.

As a retired teacher, he was intellectually compatible with me. We were in agreement on social, political, and economic issues— most of the time!

His hang-up was trying to take care of his house. He didn't like cooking and housework (he was helpless doing anything domestic). He needed someone to cook, sew, mend, iron, wash, and clean.

During the course of our friendship, he said he loved me. I felt he was really looking for a way out of his problem, especially after I saw the inside of his home. There were dirty dishes on the counters, dust on the furniture, beds unmade, and clothes draping from the chairs. Could love in this house find a way? I had visions of picking up after him the rest of my life! This should have told me something, but I was lonely. I went on with the friendship with my eyes wide open.

Just when we were getting to know each other, we ran into the real down-to-earth issues—church affiliation, financial status and unfinished grief work.

I wanted to quit our association, but he talked me out of it. He was a good man. Out of his respect and goodness to me, I reconsidered.

To begin with, we had to consider what church we would belong to—Lutheran or Catholic. Religion shouldn't have entered into the matter, but it did. We both were Christian and believed in God. However, he wanted me to belong to his church. I wanted him to belong to mine. Before we knew it, the children joined in, and the fireworks started. It was no longer a one-to-one discussion.

I told my children to stay out of it. His children took the flatter route to reach me, taking me to church events, all the time expounding the merits of their faith and church. I understood what they were trying to do. They loved their father and wanted someone to care for him.

After much soul searching, I came up with a better solution. He would go to his church. I would go to mine.

That settled, we ran into the problem of what church we would be married in.

"Here we go again," I said to Carl, feeling a bit perturbed that he wasn't seeing anything my way. "If we can't come to an amiable decision without all the hassle of the family, it's not worth it for either of us.

"Must I do all the giving in?" I asked when Carl took me home. He didn't answer, so I got out of the car and slammed the door.

Carl relented, and once more everything was peaceful between us. But it didn't last long. When we discussed which home we would be living in, the friction started all over again.

This time his children got into the act. They wined, dined, and flattered me again then expounded the merits of my living in their dad's house.

Because Carl had relented on which church we would be married in, he thought I should sell my home and move in with him. This turned me off. I felt it was unwise to live in a house occupied by a former mate. There would be too many memories—constant reminders of furniture and decorations. The thought of my sleeping in the bed occupied by his former wife turned me off.

Money and finances brought more discord to the already unsteady relationship. We held premarital meetings with the family discussing and evaluating the resources and equitable distribution of moneys and materials from the sale of his home.

This proved disastrous. The battle for rights began! The neighbors must have thought a little war was going on at his house. One son wanted the workshop tools; the other thought he was entitled to them. A daughter had to have her mother's dining room set; the other daughter said it was hers. They fought over everything except the outdated kitchen sink.

In any relationship, one has to give of oneself. He was thoughtful; I was tolerant. But the negative feelings I had through much of the relationship had to be faced and aired. I came to the conclusion that I couldn't bring companionship, affection, and supportiveness to this new relationship. I was not willing to share, care, and have genuine interest in my new partner's life. I was unwilling to make adjustments to his preferences. My problem, through it all, was that I was comparing Carl with my deceased spouse, and that was unhealthy. Andy was uppermost in my thoughts. I was not ready to trust myself to this new adventure. I could not concentrate and respond favorably to another mate at this time, especially in light of the troubles we had been having.

When we discussed our feelings, he admitted he would be marrying me to get a cook and housekeeper rather than a partner in social and spiritual activities. We agreed this would not contribute to a meaningful relationship. Insecurity, loneliness, helplessness, and inability to cope would not make our relationship a happy one. We accepted our limitations and agreed that remarriage for us would not be to our best interests. The risks would be too great.

We remained friends.

15

Living For Today

God made man and woman for each other. When death took my spouse, I felt like half a person. In marriage we had been a team, each contributing to the relationship.

Although remarriage would have solved many of my problems, I chose against it. I could not give my love and companionship to another while my deceased spouse still dominated my thinking. It would merely be an escape from loneliness. Until I had gone through the grief of widowhood—had achieved an identity of my own—I would not be capable of loving a new and different person.

This was made clear to me when Joe asked me to marry him two years after Andy's death. We had been friends for many months. He was alone and lonely, as I was. While we got along well together, I was reluctant to say yes. When he presented me with a ring, I refused. Andy was still real to me.

Andy and I had had an old-fashioned Christian marriage. He was the sole breadwinner, I the homemaker. We both believed in family life as presented in the Bible. My values were deeply rooted in personal relationships in my family. My role as mother, the heart of the family, consisted of caring for my husband, bearing and caring for the children. My joy of family sharing—loving, teaching, caring, and giving—did not depend on any recognition that I received, nor on the gratitude of those I served, nor on the love and kindness that came into my life as a result. My joy sprang from warm feelings of satisfaction and worthwhileness, from humbling, heart-lifting awareness that I was on the same footing before God. My whole life of Christian stewardship was sharing and performing. What mattered most was what our Lord thought about it. The account book of my life must therefore always be ready for audit. In return, I received love, understanding, and support from my family. I had not lived my own life—I lived through my husband. I found happiness and contentment with what I had. I would not replace marriage with a career or combine the two and be satisfied.

Amid the complexities and distractions of modern family life, many women cannot accept the emotional pressures of daily family living with its ups and downs. They feel that family life creates insurmountable obstacles that turn joy into sorrows. They find diversion in employment outside the home, making money for material possessions that seem more satisfying than home caring.

Like one friend said, "I can't stand my teenager any more. He drives me up the wall. I took a job to keep my sanity."

Now widowed, I had lost my identity as a homemaker. My grief had been a wounding, hurtful experience. My life changed so drastically. It was difficult for me, since I had known only completeness with my husband. I now had to be complete within myself in order to survive. I had to start anew to do the things I had not done before as a family member—keep accounts, know money management, and see to all the business affairs of running a home efficiently.

I soon learned that I was not an island unto myself. I needed others for the changes and any successes I had attained. I owe a great deal to those who helped me through financial matters, anger, guilt, and loneliness. At the right time, I came together with others to achieve purposes. People count. Life is a two-way street. What I put into the life of others would surely come back into my own.

God said that we are members, one of another, hand in hand, achieving, caring, and loving.

I had an experience that confounded me many times in my association with others. I understood that my wisdom was limited. I had tried to make life a little better for a couple who was confined to a wheelchair. Their sorrow in being confined made them bitter. Both refused my offer to take them to church. In the weeks that followed, I tried to show them that grief comes to all of us. I told them about losing my husband. I told them that Jesus would comfort them. He had traveled our way of life and could sympathize with them. He could be their courage when spirits are beaten and broken.

One day, after weeks of bringing them food, books to read, and clothes to wear, I read to them from *Portals of Prayer*. I read that God was most generous to all of us, both ill and well. He gave His best—His earth, His Son, His heaven. He promised:

I am with you always.

To this day, I am not sure what turned the tide and gave them a new perspective about life. Meaning and awareness came into their life. They went back to church. They were happy and cheerful when I visited them. I often wondered what it was that made the change.

71

Was it my services, my suffering in losing my husband, my belief in God and His goodness, or was it my stubbornness and persistence in never giving up on them?

In living for today, I have not always practiced what I preached. In the Sermon on the Mount, God said,

O you of little faith, do not worry about tomorrow, it will take care of itself.

At times I have been overly anxious about my material future, burdens that may or may not come about, each of which took joy and good from the day. In trying to provide adequately and achieve success, I have peered into the future, become anxious about possible obstacles and their fulfillment. This, I realize, is not using each day rightly and well.

At one time, shortly after my husband passed away, I falsely imagined that my past mistakes and failures might not be forgiven by God. It was possibly a carry-over from childhood, when I was incessantly teased, "St. Peter won't let you through the Pearly Gates. You are too much of a scamp!"

What especially helped me was my course in Psychology. Now, thoughts of the future enter my mind, but I am not anxious about them. I remember the words of Osler, who said that our duty is not to see what lies dimly in the distance, but to do what lies clearly at hand.

I learned I could bear up under burdens of each day by thinking of the smallness of today's troubles and sorrows in comparison with the sufferings of Our Lord on Good Friday. I think of the gratitude I owe Him for what He has given me. Besides, the world and God can do without me because God does not need me—I need Him!

I live in the present. I believe in today. It is all that I possess. The past is of value only as it can make the life of today fuller and freer. I have no assurances of tomorrow.

The grief that had once made me weak and vulnerable has been replaced by a peace from the absence of suffering and knowing that I have gone through bereavement and survived the ordeal.

My healing process began when I accepted the loss of my mate, when I accepted the pain and frustration that followed, and then stopped resisting them. In attempting to solve my problems, I take them to God, working my way along until I find the right replacement that works for me. Restoration came from myself and my actions—concentrating with intensity to achieve my aims. I pour spirit into my work with the bereaved, sick, and dying, making it a reflection of my faith, my integrity and ideals.

Throughout my married life I had had no time and little funds for myself. My husband and children came first. Now that I am alone, I devote time to community and church affairs, volunteer services, and becoming creatively involved with projects that interest me. Where once I cared only for my family, I now care about myself, physically and emotionally. Although my hair is graying and my face somewhat wrinkled, I accept this as a symbol of the love, care, and work I did for my family.

I must be doing something right. The other day a friend said, "You don't look your age!"

Looking back, I can see that a large proportion of the unrest, conflict, and frustration into which I fell after Andy died was due to my failure to concentrate attention on rightly using one day at a time. Yet it is natural to concern oneself about responsibilities, temptations, and problems, especially when alone and forging for oneself. It is impossible to live without hope.

I'm sure there will be new problems and troubles in my future. Living on earth is not Utopia. I do not fear the unknown, however, because I have God at my side. My ingenuity and His graces will steer me on the right course.

Many people have asked me my secret for a happy life. I have three never-failing standards to live by each day.

The first is my *Bible*. There never was or ever will be another book like it. Its pages are filled with truth which teaches me the best way of living, the noblest way of suffering, and the most comfortable way of dying. It is the guide of my journey, inspiration of my thoughts, support and comfort in life and in death. It is the only book that enlightens the world spiritually.

The second is *faith*. I have complete, unquestioning trust, confidence in God, as well as my own ability to withstand any and all principles which deviate from the norm. Someone once said that it is wisdom to believe the heart, to trust the soul's invincible surmise. My heart is led by faith. God has a purpose in my life. I have been molded in a particular way to fill a particular niche. This faith was made clear to me when I flatly refused to give allegiance to another's atheistic belief. I could never give up my Christian faith. John Greenleaf Whittier once wrote:

> The steps of faith fall on the seeming void
> But find the rock beneath.

The third is my *God* I can lean on Him when I feel lonely, fearful, worried, in danger or have sinned. He is the only great power in this universe. He gave His only begotten Son that you and I might live for all eternity. So many times He told us:

> I am your guide. Come follow me. I will go with you all the way!

My aim in life, as well as most Christians', is to have a happy death and go to heaven. I have seriously considered death, heaven and hell, and other future realities. I am only human. But I do not worry about responsibilities and problems because I have learned— the hard way—that it is unnecessary. If I give God each hour of each day by doing His will, that is all that is required of me. Unless I plow and plant in His kingdom here and now, I can forget about being with Him in heaven.

Plain, everyday goodness is the key to God's kingdom. Doers are justified before God, going forward, listening, and learning all the way. Duty is the will of God. To see work that must be done each day and not do it is a disastrous offense against God. Unless I perform divine service with every willing act of my life, I never perform it at all. What I have accomplished working for Christ lasts through the ages—throughout eternity. Is not our worth determined by the good we do?

I thank God every morning when I arise that I have something to do that must be done, whether I like it or not. I want to be a worker, not a worrier; a doer, not a deadhead; a giver, not a getter; a helper not a hinderer. No good thing is ever lost; nothing dies, not even life which gives up one form only to resume another.

My greatest joy comes not from my efforts toward self-gratification, but spontaneous service to others. Even though I am never rewarded for it, my good deed is far better than honor, riches, or pleasure.

When I saw Mary, a friend, another soul in sorrow, I felt blessed when I said, "Cheer up, friend, I passed through that affliction and trial. Our Lord sustained me, and He will you, if you trust Him." The words that were wrung from my own heart's experience made it possible for me to understand and see the need of another.

My own heart has had to ache before I could give comfort to another aching heart.

Looking back, I think of the times during bereavement when I felt utterly forsaken by God. Now I see how the trials He gave me taught me lessons of trust that I wouldn't have learned any other way.

My husband's death closed one chapter of my life and opened another. That day that he was laid to rest I had no idea what the future would hold for me, or how I was to handle it. I was left without love, hope or strength, with no one to turn to. Yet under all that trauma and fearfulness, my faith remained steadfast, even when severely challenged.

My mind wondered back to that night when an atheist said to me, "It is not God's will that Andy died," In an evening typical of a horror movie, I fought back with all the strength I could muster. I did not weaken.

Our Lord saw fit to take my cross of grief and make me stronger, as well as give me an abundance of graces to fortify myself against temporal dangers. He had made me, through suffering and trial, big enough in soul to accept trouble as a trust. He had guided me by impediments as well as successes.

No good will He withhold from those who walk uprightly.
(Psa. 84:11)

In soul searching, I recall the many friends God sent into my life, enriching my existence. I recall one in particular, Alice, who wouldn't give up on me when I was bewildered, angry, and lonely after the funeral of my husband. She stayed with me all the way. And I recall the many souls that I visited and tried to console—the sick, bereaved, and dying. In my loneliness, I needed to be busy helping others in order to survive. They were profitable hours. I recall so well the widow who so graciously said, "Thank you for caring about me. I can now go on with my life."

Since Andy's death, a whole new world has been opened up to me. I have been made richer by people—good people that I needed to make my life whole again. Out of loneliness I found love, through people from every walk of life. I have been blessed a thousandfold from dividends from my investment in people through my love, care, and concern for them.

I will not be afraid of tomorrow. God's hand is on my shoulder. The future? Why worry? God promised that if we trust Him, He will take care of every situation, no matter how trying—in His own way and time.

I felt His presence with me during bereavement. I am confident He will be with me in the future.

> With the Lord as my shepherd
> I have all that I need,
> When I follow His footsteps
> Wherever they may lead.
> He will guide, watch and keep me
> Safe, in His loving care
> While I walk through the shadows
> My Shepherd will be there.
> So when my heart is troubled,
> And I'm lost in deep despair,
> I'll dispel all my worries
> And go to God in prayer.
>
> The Author

Acknowledgments

I am indebted to *The Holy Bible*, New York Bible Society, 1867 for quotes; to Coslett Publishing Company, Williamsport, Pennsylvania, for permission to use the poem "Quietness" by Doran from *Leaves of Gold*; to Paulist Press, Ramsey, New Jersey, to quote the lines "I was revived many times . . ." by Morton Kelsey from "Afterlife"; to Harper Brothers, New York, for permission to use the lines "To lose the earth you know for greater knowing," by Thomas Wolfe, 1940.